ALFRED A. KNOPF

1915 · 100 YEARS · 2015

HOW TO WATCH A
MOVIE

HOW TO WATCH A
MOVIE

DAVID THOMSON

ALFRED A. KNOPF NEW YORK 2015

THIS IS A BORZOI BOOK
PUBLISHED BY ALFRED A. KNOPF

Copyright © 2015 by David Thomson

All rights reserved. Published in the United States by Alfred A. Knopf,
a division of Random House LLC, New York, and distributed in Canada
by Random House of Canada Limited, Toronto, Penguin Random House companies.
Originally published in Great Britain by Profile Books Ltd.

www.aaknopf.com

Knopf, Borzoi Books, and the colophon are registered trademarks
of Random House LLC.

Library of Congress Cataloging-in-Publication Data
Thomson, David, [date]
How to watch a movie / David Thomson. — First edition.
p. cm
ISBN 978-1-101-87539-1 (hardcover) — ISBN 978-1-101-87540-7 (eBook)
1. Motion pictures—Appreciation. 2. Cinematography. I. Title.
PN1994.T5295 2015
791.43015—dc23
2014046757

Jacket image: *Rear Window* (detail), 1954. Paramount Pictures
Jacket design by Oliver Munday

Manufactured in the United States of America
First Edition

For Kate, Mathew, Rachel, Nicholas, and Zachary
—I'll try not to raise the subject again

It was fairly obvious that the cinema should be my chosen means of expression. I made myself understood in a language that bypassed words, which I lacked; music, which I have never mastered; and painting, which left me unmoved. Suddenly, I had the possibility of corresponding with the world around me in a language that is literally spoken from soul to soul, in terms that avoid control by the intellect in a manner almost voluptuous.

—INGMAR BERGMAN,
on receiving the Erasmus Prize, 1965

CONTENTS

HOW TO WATCH A
MOVIE

1

ARE WE HAVING FUN?

Some people believe film critics are cold-blooded. Whereas many audiences hope to come away from a movie shaking with fear, helpless in mirth, or simply bursting with happiness, a critic sneaks away from the show, a little hunched, with a secretive smile on his face. It's almost as if the film were a bomb, or a *bombe,* an artful explosion, and the critic was a secret agent who had planted it and now takes a silent pride in the way it worked. And how it worked. Audiences believe they deserve a good time, and some feel that dismantling the machine can get in the way of the fun.

That's some people—thank God it's not you. If it were you, you wouldn't be holding me in your hand or your lap, ready to read a book about how to watch a movie. Your being here suggests you feel the process is tricky enough to bear examining. In the first sixty years or so of this medium, the cinema behaved as if pleasure was its thing, and its only thing; but in the sixty years since, new possibilities have emerged. One is that pictures are not just mysteries like *The Maltese Falcon* or *The Third Man,* but mysteries like *Blow-Up* and *Persona,* or *Magnolia* or *Amour,* which ask, well, what *really* is happening, what do these cryptic titles mean, and what are those frogs in *Magnolia* meant to be? There is something else: a wave of generations now think some movies might be as fine as anything we do, as good as ice cream or Sondheim, things you can't get out of your head, where watching (or engagement) becomes so complex and lasting that you may welcome guidance.

In the 1960s, when "film study" first took hold in academia, there were well-meaning books that tried to explain what long shots and close-ups were, with illustrations, and what these shots were *for.* Such rules were at best unreliable. They felt as if assembled by thought police, and they depressed anyone aroused by the loose *Bonnie and Clyde*–like impulsiveness on screen. I pick that film because it's symptomatic of a sixties energy in movies, a feel for danger and adventure: hang on, this is a bumpy ride, and should we be having such fun killing people? Is it a genre film about 1932 or some cunning way of talking to 1967?

I'm more interested in discussing *that* experience: the way film is real and unreal, at the same time; what a shot is, or can be, and a cut; how we work up story from cinematic information and the helpless condition of voyeurism; what sound does (its apparent completion of realism, as well as its demented introduction of music in the air); the look of money in movies (no art has ever been as naked about this, or such a prisoner to it); the everlasting controversy over who did what; and the myth known as documentary (is it salvation or just another story-telling trick?).

More than that, the ultimate subject of this book is watching or paying attention (that encompasses listening, fantasizing, and longing for next week) and so it extends to watching as a total enterprise or commitment. Driving can be fun, too, and its passionate progress resembles movies—its motion is emotional. But a driver has to watch not just driving, but the road, the light, the weather, and the unexpected action of strangers. So as well as discussing movies, I will speculate on reading, looking at paintings, watching wildlife at the beach, or the wilder life in people close to you, and the total matter of how we see ourselves in life. It comes to this: a hundred and fifty years ago, people lived a life and referred it to books, games, and works of moral instruction. But in the time since then we have acquired this mechanism that mimics the way we attend to the world as a whole. Often enough, it supplants living, to say nothing of moral instruction. So we watch, but we watch ourselves watching.

Think of these models: there is watching as surveillance, or bearing dispassionate witness: you see waves breaking on the shore; you see flowers bloom and wither; you see your own infants become adults. This watching takes years; it lasts out your life. And it dismisses most schemes of judgment, even if that lesson takes time. But then something happens in the spectacle: one wave coming in bears a body—is it a corpse or a mermaid? That flower you're seeing is picked by a good-looking person. Your child is doing something dangerous. The melodrama of story begins, and movies cling to melodrama.

Once upon a time, movies had elementary and appealing mysteries or quests in their shape. Like "the lost girl." So many movies had that mythic pursuit: in *Way Down East*, Lillian Gish plays a fallen woman—can she be rescued? In *Sunrise*, Janet Gaynor is a wife on the edge of being murdered—will she be saved? In *City Lights,* the tramp loses the blind girl once she can see. In *Casablanca,* Ingrid Bergman was lost to Humphrey Bogart, but here she comes again—can she save him? In *Out of the Past,* Mitchum loses Jane Greer, but then he has the bad luck to meet her again. *Gone Girl* is about a wife who has vanished, leaving the husband to explain the black hole.

Then something shifted in the potential of the myth, as movies became more searching. Finding the girl, or saving her, was no longer a simple means to happiness. In *Vertigo,* Jimmy Stewart falls in love with a lost soul, and loses her, but then her twin appears—is this to save him or destroy him? In *L'Avventura* a woman goes missing and we search for her . . . until we forget the search because there is a new woman. In *Persona,* a great actress stops dead one night onstage—and a nurse takes her over. In *Chinatown,* the full tragedy hits when the lost girl is rescued. And then in Luis Buñuel's *That Obscure Object of Desire,* a man's search for a magical woman is confounded because there are two of her. (The way there were in *Vertigo?*) That's a brief history of the movies in which the message is not just "aren't movies fun?" but "are you watching closely enough?"

You'd better be, because these days, as you know, a carefree state of mind usually means you are being watched.

There are so many ways of watching—and so many definitions of what a movie might be. You can observe as a helpless onlooker, even one as neutral or powerless as a camera. But when the camera's detached record is examined, many watchers may say, "Look—look at the power of the camera!" Sometimes to understand that power we have to watch someone watching.

Already, I've used words that require attention. Take "fun" as a starter. It's the automatic assumption of many people still that we go to the movies for "fun," though others say the "entertainment" industry has done its best in the last few decades to kill that habit. But "entertainment" is another tricky word. It easily translates into having or being given "a good time," and over its history the business has described that as escapism, relaxation, getting away from real life and its insoluble problems for ninety minutes—taking it easy in the midst of a life that can be unbearable.

In Preston Sturges's *Sullivan's Travels* (1942), we meet a very successful Hollywood director, John L. Sullivan (Joel McCrea), who has had hits like *Ants in Your Pants of 1939*. But he's troubled—the look of vexation on McCrea's swell face is one of the film's first comic delights. He wants to be serious, to have respect and . . . books written about him? He yearns to encounter real life and put its tough tales on screen. So he dresses up as a hobo and goes on the road. To cut a long story short, he ends up sentenced to six years on a chain gang in the South. (Hard stuff now—worse in 1942.)

His life there is grim and without prospects. But on Sunday the prisoners are taken to a nearby church for a movie show. They see a Disney cartoon, starring Pluto, and Sully starts to laugh along with the other no-hopers and feel better.

Now, Sturges is a great director, and this film is a merry satire on Hollywood and pretentiousness, as well as a sweetly organized comedy. Moreover, it was made at a desperate time across the world in which the relief of movies was as treasured as it has ever been. And there is Sturges warning filmmakers against undue gravity and self-importance. Why not let the chumps laugh and have a good time? I like that attitude (I was born in 1941 and grew up in a strange nostalgia for the war and its uneasy deal with happiness), and I still cling to the hope that there can be good movies that entertain nearly everyone without being stupid or dishonest.

Don't forget that, even in 1940–45, the world was making some of its best and most enduring pictures—*The Shop Around the Corner* by Ernst Lubitsch; *The Lady Eve,* another Preston Sturges picture; *His Girl Friday* and *To Have and Have Not* by Howard Hawks; *The Letter* by William Wyler; *The Maltese Falcon* by John Huston; *Laura* by Otto Preminger; *Meet Me in St. Louis* by Vincente Minnelli.

Those Hollywood pictures easily qualify as "entertainments" and they were all popular successes. But the list can be expanded to include riskier ventures from dangerous times and other countries: *Henry V* by Laurence Olivier; *Rome, Open City* by Roberto Rossellini; *Les Enfants du Paradis* by Marcel Carné; *The Life and Death of Colonel Blimp* by Michael Powell and Emeric Pressburger; *Les Dames du Bois de Boulogne* by Robert Bresson; and even *Citizen Kane* by Orson Welles. Not all of those were hits, or comfortable to watch. Yet they have passed into history as classics because enough people have become accustomed to expecting films to be more than fun. They might be art, too. Don't be put off by that word: art can be appealing and informing (another word for entertainment). It can be fun, too.

Not that "fun" covers film in the war years adequately. In 1945, British and American military film crews went into concentration camps that had just been liberated: Bergen-Belsen, Dachau, Buchenwald. Russian crews had been at Auschwitz. The footage shot in those places was not fun, yet it was reasonable to say it demanded to be seen. Film has that power: seeing can be believing. Under Sidney Bernstein of the Psychological

Warfare Division, the British planned a filmed report to be called "German Concentration Camps Factual Survey." Alfred Hitchcock was one of the professionals called in to help on the project. The footage is hideous, terrifying, and the record of a turning point in human history, as well as necessary evidence. It is worse than anything you have seen before, yet absolutely essential.

Then, in the recovery effort after the war, the authorities determined that the planned film risked upsetting viewers and deterring progress and reconciliation. So it was shelved. The material would not be seen widely until 2014, when André Singer released *Night Will Fall*, a documentary that describes the 1945 attempt. It is still something everyone should see, and watch and talk about.

There are situations in our lives where the way we watch the world may be necessary for the continuation of life. *How to Watch a Movie* is a guide to studying film, and having more fun and being more moved. But watching is a defining part of citizenship, a bearing witness. Ordinary Germans who lived close to the camps elected not to "see" them. Some of the most striking scenes in *Night Will Fall* are of those citizens being marched through the stench, the horror, and the neighborliness of the camps. If you can't or don't watch, you have no chance of knowing what is happening, and film—in all its uses—offers some prospect of seeing the facts. For while the camera is a machine, you are not.

These days, a movie can be as short as ninety seconds, and you may find it just four inches by three on your computer. I am going to propose in this book that our old defnition of "a movie" is nearly worn out. For decades, we had a shared sense of the word: a movie was something made, advertised, playing at your local theater; it was ninety minutes (once), and now it is over two hours; it tells a story according to certain conventions we all used to understand. But now . . .

Well, those conventions are in turmoil, and a lot of people don't actually go to see "a movie," but they watch movie, or moving pictures, which can be a friend making faces at you on an iPhone, television commercials, some weird twenty-second dream you find on the Net; or the eighteen-inning game between the Giants and the Nationals (2014), which has an apparent unity or story, but is also a chaos of fragments because of the ads, the graphics, and the slow-motion analyses. All of this and much more counts as "movie."

I was arguing with a friend as to whether Columbia University should confer an honorary degree on Derek Jeter, the longtime shortstop for the New York Yankees who was then nearing the climax to his farewell season, 2014. My friend felt Jeter was a natural candidate; I was less sure, even if my doubts were fixed on the rationale behind honorary degrees as a whole. But then another friend asked if I had seen Jeter's Gatorade spot. I went to YouTube for one of the most artful pieces of moviemaking of the year.

It is a small movie, and as old-fashioned as Tyrone Power, in black-and-white, and shot on a fine summer day. The "golden" patina of the imagery suggests well-being, contentment, and humidity-free bliss. This is added to by a persistent stress in the imagery so that it keeps surging from right to left in terms of camera movement, its line of action or the destiny of its hero. These devices have been used in movies for a hundred years, though some viewers hardly notice them because they are emotionally transported by their momentum.

The character here is Derek Jeter—tall, still young, with a shaved head, a simple collarless shirt, and an easygoing, genial regard. He is in a cab, on his way to a game at Yankee Stadium (a trip he has made thousands of times, if seldom in a cab). Then he stops the driver and says he'll walk the rest of the way.

I'm not sure how often Derek has done this in life, and I'm sure that on his journeys to the park Frank Sinatra's "My Way" was not playing in the air. But Sinatra's assurance now harmonizes with the warmth of the image and the thrust of its direction.

People notice Jeter—he is famous all over the country, never mind in the Bronx. He smiles, nods, and speaks to fans—I should say that I have no reason to suppose Derek Jeter is anything but a lovely, decent guy.

The song builds. He enters the clubhouse. He puts on the pinstripe uniform. He is about to go on the field. He reaches up to touch the inscribed motto, from Joe DiMaggio, "I want to thank the Good Lord for making me a Yankee," and then as seen from behind and at a reverent low angle, he is in the open air of the packed stadium, lifting his hand to acknowledge the worship. There is even a moment when he nods at our camera as if to say, I knew you were there all along. And we realize—because this has been going on all our lives—that something else is coming, like the insignia "G" for Gatorade, in color. The farewell tribute to maybe the best shortstop in history (his numbers vie with those of Honus Wagner and Cal Ripken) has been an advertisement. And that leaves us as suckers.

Jeter is a Hall of Fame player and he has had his rewards: money, to be sure (his net worth is estimated at $180 million); the honest affection of fans; ample victory; a career with one club; and an unflawed reputation—something not common in athletics these days. But, I asked my friend, suppose the ad had been set on the campus of Columbia, with Jeter accepting the tribute of students and faculty, because he had decided to walk, would that strengthen or diminish his case for an honorary degree? Or would the process of commerce and aggrandizement in the filming begin to compromise a great university?

Perhaps, instead, the maker of the film deserves something. Perhaps he or she graduated from the film program at Columbia?

I pick on this mini-movie because it is wonderfully done, yet ultimately depressing, and because it supports a large part of my argument—that to watch movie properly you have to watch yourself watching.

Am I being hard on the "fun" of this little promotion? It had two million hits in a trice on YouTube and many people felt it was grand and cheering. Why shouldn't New Yorkers and the rest of us feel good about Derek and his modest charm? Well, if you felt uplifted when you saw the ad, nothing I say will erase that. But the stir of the Sinatra song (a testament to willfulness) and the texture of the imagery put me in mind of another exceptional piece of movie. I am thinking of the arrival by air in Nuremberg of Adolf Hitler in Leni Riefenstahl's inspiring but despised "documentary" of 1935, *Triumph of the Will.* If you think that's going too far, take a look (it's on YouTube, too). The sunlight, the hallowed black and white, the motion, the accumulation of music and the crowd, and the strangely meek persona of these gods—the ingredients are similar. Plus this: *we* are watching and being carried along.

Filmmakers like to say that newsreel and documentary are sacred or inviolable. But in so much of what we see now the sacred has been infiltrated by commercialism, propaganda, and the way history is turned into fiction.

2

SCREENS

Screens are strange tools; they display and they conceal. After all, film screens are the bearers of revelation, and so we get most of our murders and our naked people on them like omelettes we cannot eat. But sometimes in life as much as in movies, a screen is the means of dainty concealment where women retreat to disrobe. In *Rio Bravo,* Feathers (Angie Dickinson) goes behind one to take off the tights her sheriff disapproves of. Screens are equivocal as furniture and inflammatory safeguards. And they are increasingly present in our lives. Ask yourself how many hours a day you are dealing with a screen, and remember how shocked we were to learn that our children were taking in six hours of television a day by 1960.

If you'd seen *Sullivan's Travels* in 1942, it would have involved walking to a movie screen in your neighborhood. You knew what was playing because you had passed the theater itself, the shell that held the pearly screen. You might have read advertisements in local papers, or had a film recommended by word of mouth. So you went out, and to this day the archaic business hopes that audiences are still lured by that impulse, no matter that many of us carry a screen around in our pocket and have a far more complicated sense of being "in" or "out."

So you went to purpose-made buildings called cinemas. They had names like Palace, Plaza, Regal, Odeon, Astoria, Lux, Imperial, Electric, Granada, and they were lustrous, seductive, romantic, comic. (Those names are full of nostalgia now—whereas if the movies were a brand-new business, the venues would have different names: the Cut, FX, Scream!, Murder, Chase, Naked, iScreen . . . all suggestions welcome.) The old movie houses were the most gaudy and enticing premises on the high street when I was growing up in England. Most shops were drab after the war, while the churches were reproachful. The cinema was fragrant—there was perfume in the air, though maybe that was meant to kill the germs. The place was fulsomely designed: there were Egyptian, Aztec, Moroccan, Oriental, Spanish moods, and they were as inaccurate historically as the costume romances and adventure pictures that were playing—*Captain from Castille, Son of Ali Baba, The Flame and the Arrow.*

In the bigger urban theaters, in America as well, there was carpeting on the floor and the seats were upholstered. In the evenings especially, you had to be there early if you wanted to get in. *About half the population went once a week.* Every moviegoer of that era knew the experience of being turned away; it was a disappointment but it made the picture show more desirable. Most of the time until at least the early 1950s, the place seemed packed. Usherettes with flashlights might have found you the odd single seat, so you sat in dense rows, among strangers, united by the cigarette smoke and the palpable anticipation.

The prize theatre in my part of south London was the Granada, in Tooting, which had grottoes and chapels fit for Moorish Spain (or a Hollywood Moorish Spain). I would have guessed that theatre held 2,000 people, and I was there often when every seat was sold. But I looked it up and the actual capacity was 3,000. So I saw the daft, bronze statue named Victor Mature and the writhing, devious Hedy Lamarr as *Samson and Delilah* there (and became anxious about going to the barber), with 2,999 strangers, and we were—more or less—as one. That is a hard ecstasy to abandon.

I do not know the exact dimensions—I am estimating them from an old photograph. But I am guessing that the curtained screen at the Granada was thirty feet high by sixty feet wide, bigger than houses in the surrounding streets. From a booth high up in the back of the auditorium reels of film were projected onto this white screen using a high-power carbon arc lamp. A reel ran for ten minutes, so two 35 mm projectors stood side by side, and relied on a projectionist who saw the reel-change blobs in the top right-hand corner of the image and knew to start the second projector. It was a feat of magic, technology, and craft to run a movie smoothly and keep it in focus without a projector bulb burning out. These projectors now are scrap, and the profession of projectionist is dying away. You knew this, but you may not know the love or pride that went into it, or the rapture that gripped the crowd, whatever the film was.

Cinema was a light show, no matter the stress on stars and stories, and that's not so different from the technologies it yielded to. When television came along, it was a light that was turned on. You could walk down a suburban street at night and see the same steely glow of attention or worship burning in so many houses, without burning them down. Even at a cinema these days, with a fair to middling crowd, you may see downcast faces lit up by glowworm iPhones everywhere. We love the light—just think of the distress to the culture at large, let alone the individual, if the light didn't come on. This reliance leaves us so vulnerable. The frustration in a movie theater if a film "breaks down" is one thing. But if all our computers and iPhones failed to ignite, the terror of being "down" and of an ensuing chaos is such that we may realize why so many of us have guns. (I mean Americans.)

Audiences told themselves they were seeing stories couched in an astonishing lifelike illusion, but the technology was as profound as fiction's magic. That truth has become more pressing as screens have become ever more active and assertive. The modern acceptance of IMAX and 3D has surpassed the way, for decades, 3D was offered by the business but dismissed by public confidence that stories counted. Yet watching Derek Jeter on YouTube in 2014 is not so different from watching *Sullivan's Travels* at the Palace in 1942. The same curious and largely unexamined role of the screen obtains. Jeter is small—I said three inches by four—but kids seem captivated by smaller images still. Is it possible that they are not quite looking, but feeling "in touch"?

When I look at YouTube I am trusting to an invisible agency. If I had to explain it to you in the way I explained movie projection, I would sound vague: I turn on my machine, my computer; I punch in YouTube, and ask for "Derek Jeter Gatorade," and his little movie leaps into being. I might tell you or a young child, well, it's instant electronic communication, it's tapping into a data bank, it's the Internet. I don't know how it really works; that's why I'm in trouble if it ever goes wrong. But it also means I am cut off from the process itself. You may say I'm too old or too dumb to possess a complete explanation, but I don't think I'm alone. And that mystery is significant. When I first went to the movies, I was entranced by the "reality" on screen. I believed there must be people behind or within the screen. My father made an airy, passable explanation of what was happening. He pointed to the window in the projection booth and the beam of light aswirl with cigarette smoke. I could trace the physical process—and I have never lost my affection for projectionists. Whenever it was possible, I loved being in the booth, seeing the cans of 35 mm film, looking at the fleshy celluloid loops in the projectors, and feeling the heat and energy of those machines.

There is so much more absence and liberty with YouTube (or its variants). I get through to what I want (as if making a telephone call), but I don't have to watch or attend to it. I can take a phone call, eat a slice of pizza, romance my girl (or the dog). The film is my plaything or my pet, whereas a movie was like a beast that dominated me. An old movie was a matter of size and illumination in which faces might be thirty feet high (and watching movie is a face-to-face interaction, so don't forget the disparity of scale). The film had a life or momentum of its own. It drove on relentlessly, and I soon realized that the image could change from x to y quicker than I could close my eyes, when x might be John Sullivan in his elegant Beverly Hills home and y was something closer to the liberation of Bergen-Belsen. In all likelihood, I was in a row of occupied seats: if I was distressed (and I was often upset and in tears when I first went to movies), it was fuss and embarrassment to get up, to say excuse me to all those strangers, and try to get out of that place.

There are other liberating limitations to Jeter on YouTube, or whatever you have selected there. When my choice comes up, it is one among so many other things the system says it can show me. So I am distracted as I start to watch. I may give up Jeter after twenty seconds and move to some of the other resources and opportunities my very basic computer can bring me. It's churlish of me to complain, because I know the Internet is my window on the wide world. And it's not as if I haven't had happy or diverted hours flitting from Kim Kardashian to Susan Sontag. I don't decry the infinity of a civilization where I can summon up Derek Jeter, the text of a story by Borges, the latest piece of hardcore pornography, the vital statistics of Sierra Leone, or that diner conversation between De Niro and Pacino in *Heat*. But the sheer range can be disturbing or depleting. The determining impulse in marriage, say, or falling in love, lies in meeting one person at a time. But when so many possibilities exist, then maybe marriage and love itself come to be less urgent or convincing.

If we lament attention deficit disorder in our children, we should admit the dissolution of attention (or watching) in our own technologies. If that sounds too general, think of the agencies—from individuals and businesses to governments and ideologies—that would prefer us not to attend with too much critical concentration, but let the passing spectacle swim by without challenge.

This is where watching cannot rest with mere sight. It waits to be converted into aesthetic judgment, moral discrimination, and a more intricate participation in society. That sounds ominous, I suppose, and part of a creeping unease at how the Internet can be a spectator sport that condones our lack of concentration and begins to deepen feelings of futility over dealing with the world. In that mood, there are film commentators who lament the loss of the large screen, the locomotive of the movie, and our amazed attention to it all. Things have been lost, but now I have to make the most challenging point—that cinema, film, movie (whatever) always had the seed of dislocation about it.

The novice at the movies is often overwhelmed by the reality of it all. When Auguste and Louis Lumière showed pieces of film to a paying audience in Paris in December 1895, it is said that some customers ran from the salon screaming because they believed a steam engine coming gently toward the camera would break out of the screen and strike them. Were they pretending? Perhaps they were unsure. "Primitive" peoples shown close-ups of the face are sometimes fearful that decapitation has occurred. When I saw Olivier's *Henry V* at the age of four, I "saw" the faces of page boys in the English camp at Agincourt on fire. It was one of the occasions on which I had to be carried away in tears. Later on, I realized I was reacting to a dissolve— the faces and the fire had been laid together. Anyone poised on the edge of a miracle is "primitive" and vulnerable to the uncertainty: is this the real thing or a trick?

The spectacle of real shock never loses its power—those piled corpses at Dachau and their helpless abandon are testament to that, along with our creepy readiness for real disaster (so long as it stays on the screen). That first Lumière film show was a treasury of ordinary events being brought to the eyes of millions: the train entering a station; workers leaving a factory; a family having a picnic. The films made by Georges Méliès in France after 1895 are from another reality—that of imagination. They have enormous charm, still, but I don't think they match the unconsidered naturalism of the Lumière films. Whereas Méliès had the cunning ingenuity of a stage magician who had discovered film as a new toy, the Lumières had no other plan except to prove that their machine, the *cinematographe,* worked.

In 2014, the British Film Institute put together a collection of bits and pieces an audience might have seen at the movies in 1914. That was an age of fragments, shorts, snippets, jokes, mere observations, snaps, and "Look!" items. There was everything from the *Perils of Pauline* serial and a bit of Chaplin to scenes of the uneasy Hapsburg royal family and views of cheery soldiers marching somewhere. Pauline looked fussy and foolish. Chaplin seemed calculating and unkind. The marching soldiers were probably under orders for the film. There is no clue how close they were to the Western Front. There is no hint of war. But you don't forget the long-suffering lean faces of the soldiers, just as the impatience of the Hapsburgs is a clue to their disastrous superiority. There are views of Egypt and the Pyramids, as ravishing as the footage Herbert Ponting shot in 1911–12 when he accompanied Captain Scott on his expedition to the South Pole. "Ravishing" does not mean simply that those compositions are beautiful—though they are a picturesque vision of Antarctica waiting meekly for man's conquest (which was not how it turned out, as Scott and four others perished). What is most arresting is how people had never seen such things before. There is wonder, information, and relationship in seeing an emperor's pale, pinched face, the North African desert, or the surreal devastation at Fukushima in March 2011. Do you remember the flooded multistory car park there and the automobiles reversing in the rush of water like obedient toy cars? In such cases, the horror and the beauty are closely aligned. In the Dachau footage, the obscenity of those reduced human corpses does not erase the sheer beauty of any body. The scene is one of torture and murder, but it might make Francis Bacon or Egon Schiele giddy.

The honesty of that complicated response stemmed from the immediacy of photography, and for several decades little got in the way of that transaction. Audiences were dazzled to see the elemental life of an eskimo in *Nanook of the North* (1922), Robert Flaherty's pioneering documentary, to see the mute grace of Gary Cooper in so many films, and to observe the delicate tour de force of Fred Astaire in which this very modest man was able to do such difficult things with grace and unbroken fluency.

The awe-inspiring circumstances in which cinema was enjoyed only added to the overwhelming illusion of a reality to be beheld and participated in vicariously. It was an open and largely unexplored question how audiences were meant to reconcile that level of reality with the apparatus of fantasy. Yes, Fred could dance like that—but we couldn't. De Niro and Pacino might chat forever over coffee, liberating our fantasy that cops and hoods are brothers from the same acting school. John Wayne could be the indomitable heroic figure in so many adventures—in the West, in the war, even in the green fields of Ireland—but we had a harder time sustaining the heroic interpretation of our own lives. We were encouraged to make a contract in our lives in which hard times were offset by fantasy success. Wayne's glory was our ghostly purchase, and it was only later that we learned how thoroughly he had missed war service.

That screen contract began in the movies and became the engine of advertising. For there is a dreamed assumption in the Jeter Gatorade ad not just that Derek walks like a god on earth (he may not share that feeling—we don't care), but that ordinary people in the Bronx will be beatified and saved by contact with him. In *Triumph of the Will,* when Hitler is driven in an open car from the airfield through the packed streets of Nuremberg, his car halts and a mother and child come forward from the crowd to greet him. This was meant to seem spontaneous or natural, yet plainly it was staged. Then, as the humble couple meet the Führer and step back they go from shadow into sunlight. Their radiance is real—just a mother and child on the street in the sun—but they existed then, and now, in the theater of fascism.

Riefenstahl understood how these mechanisms worked. If that is her largest "crime" or cynicism, it's one she could have learned from American films, where the use of light to ennoble some characters was automatic and constant. It's a lesson in the DNA of those who made the Jeter ad, too, yet few of the audience know how to read the contrivance and the manipulation of what seems like wholesome imagery. We have been fools not to teach this way of reading in a culture in which for decades most children have spent more time watching moving imagery than reading books.

But a change has occurred, in which the technological impediments in film have compromised our contact with reality. This subversive force cannot be omitted in any talk about how to watch a movie. Yes, the screen seems to be a window on paradise in which we are the beneficiaries. But context has been betrayed. We are *not* there, with the spectacle; we are in this odd, privileged position of secret onlookers. We are in a dark and an isolation which suggests our weakness for fantasy. The screen is a window, but a barrier, too, and one that consigns us to a kind of purposeless oblivion.

Let me explore the existence of *Heat* (1995) on screen a little further. As written and directed by Michael Mann, it is an absorbing picture, a suspenseful narrative for its full 171 minutes. I watch it a lot, and I can tell myself it is for the craft, the art or the performances (it is one of De Niro's last good pictures). But I know I am drawn to it by the licensed fantasy of watching alleged cops and robbers strutting their stuff—with guns, but with talk, too. It is a potent male dream. The women in the film are often intriguing, but they are not permitted to rival the male ideology. And *Heat* is a fire that doesn't burn me. I can watch its immense street gun battles with excitement; I can be carried away by the notion that De Niro and Pacino are alike in their characters. But my wife once was mugged and I know that that suggestion of parity is insane. A brush with violent crime in life can be searing and traumatic. Yet on screen it is indulged. Film only works in the dark, and because of that safe distance from life.

The intrinsic deal in the movies was to say, Look, for a very modest sum—a nickel, say—we'll give you an opportunity to see not just the wonders of the world, not just people who are beautiful beyond your dreams, but a set of conditions to which we know you aspire: sexual splendor, thrilling violence, clothes, décor, space, timing, and ultimate happiness; in short, the chance to bathe in the light. It's the treat of the new age, and here's the kicker: you can watch the sex and violence without ever being identified, or known. The beautiful men and women will come right up to the screen and gaze into your darkness alight with desire and availability. They may start to slip off their clothes and their inhibitions. But they won't notice you. They won't cry out, "Peeping Tom!" and shame you. Your voyeur rapture will be condoned. You can cough or sigh and the music of the movie will smother the guilty sounds. There's only one drawback: you can't come up on screen or pass through the window. You stay in the dark. You are invisible, anonymous; you are part of the mass for a medium made of light.

Historically, it is still a great puzzle, yet one can try to track the consequent disillusion. I suspect it started with sound, for that enhancement of the love of reality does seem to have wiped out a great deal of innocence. Consider Fritz Lang's first sound film, *M* (1931).

Lang was a visionary of silent cinema, audacious and ambitious, and possessing one of the greatest composing eyes the medium has ever known. He had done *Siegfried* and *Kriemhild's Revenge* as parts of Wagner's *Die Nibelungen*; in *Dr. Mabuse, the Gambler* he had created one of the most spectacular mad genius criminals of the age; in *Metropolis,* he had delivered a future society in which the precious few lived in penthouse light while the masses labored underground. In *Woman in the Moon* he had broken into science fiction. Then in 1931, he and his wife, the screenwriter Thea von Harbou, noticed a rash of serial killings in Germany. They asked themselves, How can you make a movie about a serial killer?

Lang remembered a stage actor he had seen a few years earlier in Berlin in Wedekind's *Spring Awakening.* He was short, squat, and so far from conventionally handsome it was disturbing. You could not take your eyes off him, just as his own popping eyes seemed to feed on anything he looked at. He was close to grotesque, and yet he was funny, amusing, dreamy, and in some lights he had the face of a wounded angel. He was a phenomenon; Lang had seen no one like him, and cinema has always wanted to show us things never seen before. His name was Peter Lorre. Lang approached him and asked, "You have done a movie?" Lorre said he had not, and the director made him promise he would not do a picture before Lang put him in one. "Of course," said Lorre, "but what film is this?" I don't know yet, said Lang.

So Lorre became Hans Beckert in a film intended to be called "Murderers Among Us" until Lang had the brainwave of branding simplicity—call it *M,* for that insolent panache refused to be daunted by the dark material. Wasn't there a key moment in the film when a blind beggar identified Beckert—because he was whistling a theme from Greig's *Peer Gynt* (this was a sound film)—and then another street criminal scrawled a white chalk M on the palm of his hand and slapped it on Beckert's shoulder? That allowed one of the famous shots in film history where Beckert looks in a mirror and sees the M on his back (like a frightened man gazing at a screen).

M is a classic now, among our great films, but it was unprecedented in pushing the regular process of audience identification to a new limit. Beckert kills children. You know you are against that. In 1931, it was not possible for a movie to show that action—today, we have become more sophisticated and tolerant. But there is an alarming moment in Lang's film where he cuts to a sudden close-up of Beckert taking a knife from his pocket. He flicks it open—and peels an orange for a little girl. Even now, it's ample suggestion; in 1931, it must have been more frightening still (we all know that moment when we guess a film is going to show us something so awful we may not be able to watch).

In the 1931 movie, the child killer is such a disturbance to organized crime that the underworld hunts the killer along with the police. He is captured at last and accused in a mock trial staged by the criminals. Beckert breaks down and admits to his irresistible impulse—he is crazy, but he can explain it. He may be the most appalling movie killer shown to that time, but he is the one who makes the most insidious appeal for sympathy in which the pathology of the murderer is infernally tangled with Lorre's eloquence as an actor.

I suspect the piercing shot of Beckert seeing himself in the mirror (or on a screen) was instinctive on Lang's part, but he was a fervent psychologist of screen dynamics, and he created imagery with the spontaneity of a poet—albeit a cold one. The image speaks to the new ambiguity that *M* has uncovered and the way we are gazing at, and beginning to want to understand, a figure who would be alien and alarming in most circumstances. Suppose at a screening of *M* in Berlin a man had been caught attacking a child in the audience, mob fury would have descended on him without mercy (and Lang was very good on mob fury). But that same audience is breaking perilous ground in contemplating Beckert's justification. The "ordinary" status of reality is being undermined by a new detachment. The dilemma will recur throughout this book, but *M* is one of the first times the slippage was clear. And it is a great film, as beautiful as it is sinister. Is that mix really possible? Or is it something cinema invented? Everyone liked *M,* from Graham Greene to Joseph Goebbels, who wrote in his journal, "Fantastic! Against humanitarian soppiness. For the death penalty. Well made. Lang will be our director one day."

The consequences are as fascinating as the film itself. For Peter Lorre, it was a breakthrough and a curse. No one in the business ever forgot his performance, or believed he should depart from it. He felt imprisoned by the assumption that he was perfect casting as a murderer. About two years after the movie was made, in the spring of 1933, Lang was called in for an interview by Goebbels. The new head of propaganda and the Führer himself had been thrilled by Lang's pictures. So they wanted him to take charge of film for the Third Reich. Not long thereafter (though not as swiftly as he claimed later), Lang left Germany (Lorre quit, too). They went their separate ways to Hollywood, yet never worked together again. As for *M,* it was some time before its insights flowered—for censorship stood in the way to protect us. But over time the medium shrugged that off, and so we were in for a run of extraordinary films and shows: *Psycho* (no director learned more from Lang than 'Hitchcock), *The Godfather, The Silence of the Lambs, Se7en, The Girl with the Dragon Tattoo* . . . *The Sopranos, Dexter, Breaking Bad.*

That's too dark a view? How many real killings have you seen? I'm guessing and hoping very few—zero perhaps. And how many have you seen presented and pretended to on some screen? Well, if you're thirty and American, the number is around thirty thousand. Does that imbalance amount to an attention disorder?

3

ALONE TOGETHER?

In the last chapter, I was treasuring the community of film-going in the late 1940s. But I wonder if I was being unduly sentimental or nostalgic, for I know in my innermost being that another thing that has always appealed to me about the movies is the solitude, or the aloneness, they foster. How can those reactions coexist?

The community wasn't simply a mythic idea promoted by the business. Moviegoing was the national pastime. By the late twenties, a third of Americans were going to the pictures once a week. In the war years, that figure reached 70 million admissions on a population of about 140 million. Immediately after the war it was 80 million—or still half the population. The average admission price was less than 50 cents. The theaters were crowded or packed. People went in groups and they saw friends there. The spirit of the war was reinforced by the movies and enshrined by them. It was in theaters that we formed our idea of what war looked like, granted that the newsreels were carefully controlled and very positive. But the mood of the audience was already in favor of the war and these regular gatherings for entertainment focused team spirit as well as the pathos of those who were "away" or in danger.

Meet Me in St. Louis (1944) is set in 1904, and it delights in the prettiness of period clothes and an idealized home built on the M-G-M lot in Culver City. We meet three generations of the Smith family all living in the same house. They are excited about the World's Fair coming to St. Louis, but then a fresh adventure appears on their horizon. Alonzo, the father, is offered an important new job in New York City. If he accepts it, the family must move, and suffer the disruption and transience that many regard as characteristic of American life. But then comes Christmas Eve (the picture opened in November 1944). The teenage Esther (Judy Garland) sings to her sleepless kid sister, Tootie (Margaret O'Brien), "Have Yourself a Merry Little Christmas" as they look out at the backyard with the snowmen they have built,

The song is one of the most beautiful and melancholy in the American songbook (by Ralph Blane and Hugh Martin), and the film and its director, Vincente Minnelli, use it to bring a tear to our eye—an honest tear and an innocent eye. Tootie is so torn about leaving St. Louis that she rushes down to the yard in her nightgown and destroys the snowmen. This is an M-G-M musical, but still it is one of the best domestic moments in American film. The father hears and sees this, and on the spot he quenches his own ambition and his urge to move. The Smiths will stay in St. Louis. There's no place like home. (It was the same message as delivered in another Garland film, *The Wizard of Oz*—and so the war was bookended.) But surely Alonzo is more alone amid togetherness.

The American home had not been bombed—think of the education if it had. But American families had been split apart, and here was a film that reassured the troops overseas (they were an extra audience on top of the domestic box office) that home would still be there waiting for them and their old life would resume. Those were white lies, and anyone shrewd enough would have guessed that. But the audience wanted to believe in stability, persistence, and the war being worthwhile. So the movie houses were home away from home, and strongholds of a positive and conservative state of mind.

Meet Me in St. Louis would have played with a newsreel, a couple of cartoons maybe, and a nice war bond display in the lobby. The prints of those movies still bear the legend "Buy War Bonds as You Leave This Theatre." It was a good place to be. The best time I saw my parents together—or the only time—was when they took me to the movies. This was the audience that even the rebellious John L. Sullivan reconciled himself to after a spell on the chain gang.

Moreover, the war years made classics: the history goes from *Gone With the Wind* to *The Best Years of Our Lives,* and along the way it takes in *Casablanca, Road to Morocco* (a bigger hit than *Casablanca* and equally uninterested in North Africa), *Meet John Doe,* and *To Have and Have Not.* These are emblems from a golden age eager for comfort, and it's easy to assume that they conform to the code of the happy ending. But that's not the case. Scarlett O'Hara is actually left alone, and we reckon she deserves it. *The Best Years of Our Lives* is wholesome and decent and it trusts to the good nature of ordinary people, but it admits how greed and opportunism had flourished in the war. In *Casablanca* our guy gives up his girl for higher causes. *Meet John Doe* is not just rueful, it's close to ruined in its feeling for hysteria within the American dream. *Road to Morocco* knows that Hope and Crosby should never trust one another. The only one of those classics with an unequivocally serene ending is *To Have and Have Not,* which has Bacall shuffling off with Bogart into a cockamamie future, and so contrary to the Hemingway novel it claims as its source. It's about as daft as the *Road* film, even if it's also more insolent, sexy, and knowing than any other wartime romance.

The rapture was short-lived. By 1950, attendance was down to 55 million people a week; by 1960, it was 30 million, or less than a sixth of the population. When the war ended there were many objections to the culture of the happy ending, for it seemed like a cruel lie as the truths of the war years were uncovered, from Dachau to the prospects for further wars in the bright light of Hiroshima. All over the world, there were promises to make cinema more "real," or more aware of the world's difficulties.

The old culture of Hollywood had many dissenters. The Supreme Court, seeing monopolistic tendencies, separated production and exhibition. The fear of a Communist presence in America fixed on the movie industry to gain public attention. There were brave new films about the movie business—aware of fear, exploitation, and madness: *Sunset Blvd., In a Lonely Place, The Bad and the Beautiful,* and even *Singin' in the Rain,* one of the cheekiest satires on Hollywood. There were also small crime films, as aware of the anxieties in America as the best pulp fiction—*Detour, Crossfire, Force of Evil.* In time, these pictures were called "film noir," which had the defect of covering up their social criticism. In *Crossfire,* about a killing in the military prompted by anti-Semitism (it was homophobia in the original book), there is a throwaway scene, barely remembered now, with Gloria Grahame and Paul Kelly, that has a contempt for life as trenchant as Jim Thompson or Nathanael West. It was West who had known in 1939, in *The Day of the Locust,* that Hollywood was a depraved and deluding cultural center that deserved to be overthrown. The doubts were there. Norman Mailer, who had done some time in Hollywood and loved movies, wrote *The Deer Park* (1955), a scathing novel so much tougher than the pained hero-worship in F. Scott Fitzgerald's unfinished *The Last Tycoon.*

But the happy ending struggled on. There are always too many movies for safe generalizations. So *Crossfire, In a Lonely Place,* and Robert Aldrich's savagely disenchanted *Kiss Me Deadly* were smothered by the blancmange of *An American in Paris, The Greatest Show on Earth, Roman Holiday, The Glenn Miller Story, Love Is a Many Splendored Thing,* and *Around the World in Eighty Days,* all the way to *Twelve Angry Men* and *Ben-Hur,* epitomes of rational, liberal optimism. Of course, by the end of the 1950s, easygoing cinema was in a losing competition with the effortless mini-movies and the sublime, recurring entertainment of *I Love Lucy* and other hits from television. Movies never stood a chance against technology and its progress and the zeal of Lucille Ball and Desi Arnaz. Those "outsiders" (failures once in the Hollywood system) were so successful they would end up purchasing the tottering studio RKO. The innocent bliss of being a movie audience (or a studio) was over.

The crowd loved the sudden outburst of *Lucy,* and it fell in love with its new piece of furniture that revolutionized the practice of watching moving film. There were so many things that let you know you were trying to watch (as opposed to entering a dream): the image was small and harsh, as movies strove for more color and wider screens; it came back every week, with variations on the same situation—a TV star was suddenly working five times harder than movie stars—and for *Lucy* and so many other shows there was the sound of the studio audience. The act of watching and responding was part of the experience. The medium was becoming a conscious part of the message, just as academics like Marshall McLuhan were beginning to see that the technology often surpassed the alleged core of the show—the story. Moreover, it was always a delightful, hectic puzzle disentangling Lucille and *Lucy*. In the early fifties, TV was already flirting with its own slipping reality.

A few observers were prescient. In 1950, when only 9 percent of American households possessed a television set (with laughable reception), Ray Bradbury wrote a story now known as "The Veldt." It was regarded as science fiction and it envisaged a house that is still beyond our means. The Hadley family live in their "HappyLife House." The two children, Peter and Wendy, love the nursery because its walls are screens that can play whatever scene and scenery they desire. They prefer the African veldt, with lions prowling in the distance. The parents are troubled by this obsession (profound concentration in children can alarm parents who urge the kids to *look*). A psychologist advises them to switch the nursery off and go live in the country. But the children contrive to lock their parents in the nursery, and their last awareness is that the lions are coming closer and have been feeding on human bodies. When this story was originally published in the *Saturday Evening Post* it was called "The World the Children Made."

Four years later, Graham Greene (once a film critic and then screenwriter for *The Fallen Idol* and *The Third Man*) published a story, "The Blue Film." It is set in an unnamed country, often assumed to be Thailand, where the Carters are stationed. They are midde-aged and their marriage has soured. But they have an appetite for sensation still and the husband arranges for them to see a dirty movie show. It plays on a screen "about the size of a folio volume." It must be an old print on a creaking 16 mm projector. The second film they see is more intriguing than the first, more arousing, with an odd tenderness. It involves a man and a young prostitute. The wife realizes that the man is her Carter from twenty years earlier. The wife says the film is disgusting and she can't believe what her husband did for the camera. He was in love with the girl and his wife may read that in the film. The gap between the husband and wife seems wider and more bitter, and Greene was always better at seeing lost love than the freshly discovered thing. But the wife is now "dry and hot and implacable in her desire," and after they have had sex she says, "It's years since that happened." But Carter is left empty and desolate, feeling he has betrayed his girl from the past, the lost love of his life.

That was sixty years ago, in a rundown outpost of empire with archaic projection, but Greene had felt some of the piercing ways in which film can make the past present, to say nothing of the treacherous self-awareness we have acquired in watching ourselves. Mrs. Carter may feel they are together again, but Carter has learned a new loneliness. Take that as a segue into the whole matter of whether we are alone or together at the movies.

It's hard to treat this theme without anecdotes. I waited outsde the Regal in Streatham for a girl to join me to see *Guys and Dolls*. I was fifteen, but I loved her and she never showed up. I had been dropped, and so I went in to see that musical featuring Brando, Sinatra, and Jean Simmons. In advance, I had reckoned the film was an augury of romance. I had no intention of doing more than sneak a kiss from the girl next to me; at that time I had only vague ideas of anything else that could be done. But cinemas were places of furtive romantic action. The back rows were kept for mature kids (or immature adults), and the usherette torches were a kind of police against undue abandon. There were tales of discarded underwear being swept up when the theater closed. So I concentrated on the film. You can't take notes on movies in the dark if you're holding hands.

But that only reminds us of the gravitational pull of solitude that had always existed in cinema, long before television, McLuhan, and camp self-awareness. In that awe-inspiring dark place, it used to be said that at the end of a very emotional movie the theater kept the lights down for a moment to spare us being seen in tears. The dark is enclosing, and private; it seems to offer a privileged domain of fantasy experience. If you doubt that, consider how far the close-up is a demonstration and assertion of solitude, whether it be glorious or forlorn. Whenever the camera says, "*Look*. Look at him or her. See the depth of feeling," it is warning us of the equation of watchfulness and sense. So lovers may embrace as the curtains come together, but the film's highest moments have faces looking offscreen at that person they fear or desire (or fear *and* desire). At some time in your moviegoing you should give up the screen for a moment and study the people watching, their features bathed in light. Those faces are like the ones on screen.

There are satisfying happy endings in film history, none more so than the redemption of the Bailey family and Bedford Falls in Frank Capra's *It's a Wonderful Life*. It's hard not to see a reflection on film entertainment in that poignant and endearing picture. Capra had worked away at populist assurance in the thirties, with *Mr. Deeds Goes to Town* and *Mr. Smith Goes to Washington*. Not that he always felt comfortable: in *Smith,* and above all in *Meet John Doe,* the threat to American optimism is so hard to forget that it obscures the actual endings. James Stewart's Smith and Gary Cooper's John Willoughby come so close to despair and self-destruction. Capra had had an important role in wartime documentaries and Stewart was one of the few movie stars who had seen combat. He flew bomber missions and was not far from nervous breakdown. So *It's a Wonderful Life* was an important project for both men emotionally, not least because Capra had helped form an independent production company. They felt the need for a movie about justified sacrifice and staying the course.

The story of the film takes George Bailey to the brink of suicide; his life seems to have been a failure, along with his building-and-loan association. Then the angel Clarence shows him what might have become of his family and his community if he had perished. These scenes are scary; they are film noir set down like a gravestone in the midst of romance. So George rallies and everything turns out all right. But in the decades since its first showing, it has grown easier for audiences to imagine a question mark in the title and to realize that the idyllic Bedford Falls of 1947 has turned into a Pottersville, the drab plan of heartless capitalism pursued by the town's tycoon (played by Lionel Barrymore). But George has his Mary at the end of the film—Jimmy Stewart with Donna Reed, the last hurrah of wartime spirit and one more tribute to home values. It's a wonderful life, as long as you believe it is. But just think of that story shifted to the era of 2008 and the anxieties of middle-class existence. Once upon a time *It's a Wonderful Life* was a Christmas staple, but try showing the picture to a modern young audience without rueful irony crushing nostalgia.

Are there happy endings still in our movies? Have they survived as significant items of faith, or do they now seem bogus and foolish? Life hasn't worked out that way for Tony Soprano or Walter White, and we are likely more grown up on account of that. It's hard to think of a major American movie of this century that delivers a hard-earned happy ending. In *12 Years a Slave,* Solomon Northup regained his freedom, but we are left to ponder its extent or security in the context of 1853. Nor can one expect much contentment or ease in the work of our leading younger filmmakers: the Coen brothers, David Fincher, Paul Thomas Anderson, among others. Yet Anderson's *Magnolia,* for all the disturbing details of life it uncovers, has a stoic air of constancy and persistence as embodied in its Aimee Mann songs.

It's unbecoming to take our seriousness too seriously, especially if you've pledged your life to the chance that some movies will be as good as anything you've encountered. There is a song of solitude we can sing together from the movies. Shane is one of its heroes, forever moving on, wounded yet immortal, like the wind, and as deeply opposed to domesticity. Michael Corleone is the master of his world and maybe the most effective leader in modern American film, yet he sits implacable and alone at the end of *The Godfather Part II.* In *The Third Man,* at the cemetery, Joseph Cotten and Alida Valli fail to make contact in the strangely triumphant final shot. They have been eliminated from romantic possibility. Travis Bickle, in *Taxi Driver,* yearns to make contact with others, but his alienation turns to violence and he is left enclosed in the front of his cab, haunted by his own glance in the screen called a rearview mirror. In *Letter from an Unknown Woman*, the selfish pianist is left alone because the lover whose letter he was reading is dead. So he must face the duel he planned to evade; the endgame closes in. *In a Lonely Place* settles in as a title when the Gloria Grahame character cannot face life with the incipient murderousness in Humphrey Bogart (playing a Hollywood screenwriter).

But that edginess isn't just America in the pregnant 1950s. In Dreyer's *The Passion of Joan of Arc*, the maid is isolated by the film's ecstatic close-ups: she is transcendent, on fire before her burning, and half crazy. In Jean Renoir's *The Rules of the Game*, Octave (played by the director) is left with one friend less and without the chance of love in his life. We know now that his France is poised on the brink of war, occupation, and collaboration. *Citizen Kane* is the story of a man moving toward the loneliness of life in a deserted mansion. In *The Lives of Others*, the former Stasi functionary lives on in anonymity with just a coded book dedication to tell him he was noticed. In Mizoguchi's *Ugetsu Monogatari*, the potter is left alone without a wife or a ghost to comfort him. In *Point Blank*, the Lee Marvin character goes from being the ultimate avenger to a ghost who fades into nothingness when his victory is at hand. In *Vertigo*, the detective—that idealized model of confidence and problem-solving in many American fictions—faces his own disaster and the way he has permitted the death of his beloved not once, but twice.

Vertigo (which is now, according to the *Sight & Sound* critics' poll, the best film ever made) is a mark of Hitchcock's lifelong fascination with the process of movie. For the detective in that film is a metaphor for directors (and for Hitchcock himself?) seeking to make a woman in his own image of desire. *Vertigo* was a commercial failure when it opened, and that frustrated Hitchcock, who was as fond of his rewards as he was of movie mechanics. But it is a landmark in his inclination to leave us stranded. For years he had gone along with conventional romantic harmony as a closer—it's there in his English films, and in *Rebecca, Spellbound, Notorious, Strangers on a Train* (albeit with two anemic lovers so much less interesting than Robert Walker's killer), and even in *Rear Window*. But in *Vertigo* we have the hero's failure at our feet, and in *Psycho* there are no likeable characters left at the end, so we are put in a holding cell with Norman Bates.

Sometimes a picture comes along that is not just engrossing and moving but an enactment of this thesis. Such solitude is hard to resist. Yet *Locke* (released in 2014) is a film that in outline description seems impossible, or even absurd. How can there be a movie with only a single character on screen who never gets out of his car? What sort of story or entertainment can that make? The only answer is how could there *not* be a picture in so ingeniously fashioned a situation, granted the variety of Tom Hardy as an actor and our own profound attachment to automobiles and telephones?

Ivan Locke is married, with children. He ought to be driving home in the Birmingham area to be with them and to watch a big soccer match on television with his boys. But he is not going to make that date. Nine months before, he met a woman and had a one-night stand with her. It's not that she was the new love of his life. Indeed, she seems needy to a point of desperation; on the phone she doesn't sound like his type. But she got pregnant and elected to have the baby, and Ivan has agreed to be in London for the delivery. It is a matter of honor for him in a dishonorable situation, but now he has resolved to tell his wife about it. You see, he is a soft-spoken, rational, and conscientious man who has too much on his plate—if only he could get away to a pleasant movie and relax. As he drives the hundred miles to London, trying to speak to his wife on the car phone and talking to his nervous lover, he is also caught up in his job. Ivan is a top engineer in the concrete business (probably a first in movies). On the morrow an enormous concrete drop is to be made for the foundation of a new building. He should be there, but duty is not always a straightforward master. So now he has to talk to an assistant (less than worthy or able) to make sure nothing goes wrong. There are complications that show us how diligent and resourceful Locke can be.

He is driving south on the motorway at night—the film is 84 minutes of apparently continuous time. Occasionally *Locke* cuts away from the car interior to views of the road, of cars, and the slipstream of headlights. But this is like an interval in music. The film is rigorously concentrated on the interior as Ivan talks on his car phone to half a dozen different people. You can say that Hardy is up to the task (though I believe other actors could have done well in the role). He is inventive, brilliant, sympathetic without being ingratiating—a critic's words matter less than the creation of Ivan as a careful, dutiful Welshman, speaking softly to quell mounting stress. This is a film about reason and disorder that takes no side. You can approve or disapprove of Ivan, but only because the film keeps the neutrality of a camera, and the absorbing duplicity in which we know we are watching a living person *and* a known actor.

Locke is written and directed by Steven Knight, and I give him great credit. Yet I'm not sure this is what is commonly meant by the film of a director, or auteur. Its authorship and ownership owe so much to Hardy (it was the film that established him, beyond *Bronson* or *The Dark Knight Rises,* as a major figure), but it also springs from the technology of automobiles, recording instruments, and the subsequent solitude. No film I've seen in recent years is more eloquent on where we are now, and on how alone we feel. There is little left but to watch and listen.

A great change has occurred: once masses watched a movie together; but by now we have only our screens as company.

4

SEE IT ONCE,
WATCH IT TWICE?

For most of the medium's history, movies were made to be seen once, or as many times as you could cram into a brief run. Then they were gone. But for at least thirty years now, the technology of video has turned movies into things that can be seen and seen again. They get closer to being paintings (or views through that other kind of screen, our windows), which we may live with so long they are still there after we've gone.

If you see a movie just once, that keeps faith with its being sensational, sudden, yet as drastic as a road accident. But if you go back to watch it a second time, or many more times, you're allowing that it may be art or ritual, less the same old accident than a portent and a dream. It begins to resemble things like Velázquez's painting *Las Meninas* or some of those water lilies by Monet. This is curious, because a real water lily, like those in Monet's garden at Giverny (fifty miles northwest of Paris), comes and goes. You can enjoy the white flesh and the crimson core for now, the color and scent, but you know those blooms are not long for this world (like yourself, even if you have a few minutes longer). Be careful! Look too closely at Giverny and you may tumble into the pond. There ought to be an Agatha Christie novel, *The Drowning at Giverny*, with Hercule Poirot rhapsodizing on the fatal attraction of *nymphéas*.

There will be more water lilies next season, and they will be so close to this year's blooms that you will never tell them apart. But Monet or a professor of botany would assure you that every flower is just a little different. That's a basis for art, philosophy, and gambling: people are alike, but they are unique, too. Water-lilyness seems ready to go on forever. But these lilies, the ones you're reaching out to at Giverny, they are *now*. So seize the moment. You could rewrite those several sentences with "a woman" or "a man" or "a butterfly" substituting for water lilies. This is the enchanting mystery of nature, whereas a movie is always the same, always itself. If you want it to change, your best hope is to grow older. For older people do report that some movies seem to have shifted in their meaning or flavor as those viewers become less impressed by immediacy. In three days, a perfect bouquet may become the relic of a funeral.

Las Meninas is always the same (if restoration is careful), but it presents a moment in time, as exciting and pregnant as a great movie still. You could imagine Poirot, stepping in front of the picture and saying, "It seems so calm and orderly, doesn't it—with the infanta, her maids of honor, two dwarves, and a dog, with the flamboyant D'Artagnan-like figure of Velázquez himself, carrying a brush instead of a sword, and the ghostly reflection of the king (Philip IV) and his queen in a mirror watching the painting being made. But someone in that picture will be dead in ten minutes—most hideously dead, *mes amis*."

Does that prediction hinge on the one figure Poirot missed: the elegant but slightly sinister courtier who stands sideways with each foot on a different step, looking over his shoulder at the room? He is apparently the court chamberlain. There is a readiness in everything about this man. The others seem to have posed to be painted, but he has another mission to complete. He is a suspect seen in the open doorway in the back of the room. That shaping light around him is as strong as the glow on the infanta's brow. That infanta lived on until the age of twenty-one when after having four children and several miscarriages she died. Philip lived until 1665, Velázquez the artist until 1660. But no one knows about the dog (it's a mastiff).

I'm taking a little time with *Las Meninas* and the water lilies because they embody quite distinct ways of seeing that are married in the movies. The lilies represent surveillance; they are there forever as a plant, and we can gaze upon them for as long as our forever lasts. The reverie of looking is timeless, pantheistic, and slightly inhuman. That mode is always there in the movies: whatever the rapid turns of story, we are always dwelling on, or in the existence of, Bette Davis's eyes or the curl of Bogart's lip. This is not stressing minutiae; it is identifying the crucial texture of watching movies and wanting to be that person. It is why some actors work on screen and some do not, and it speaks to some personality in existence that is more lasting than stories.

On the other hand, the much older *Las Meninas* seems more modern in an odd way because it has picked on a moment in the life of the court of Spain. It says, *Look,* I think something is happening. It is the essence of movie melodrama, and more than three hundred years later its question is still gripping.

I am talking about looking and the momentariness that breaks into life at the movies. I cannot think of a painting before *Las Meninas* in which there is so strong a feeling of something about to happen. "Next" is so alluring. Compare it with Rembrandt's *The Night Watch,* done only a dozen years earlier. That's a masterpiece and a noble spectacle, but it is an assembly of notable people, arranged so that everyone can be seen. It is posed, not poised, and as still as a tableau. Socially it is fixed in the idea these men have of being grandees. Nothing is about to happen. But in *Las Meninas* some threatening future shivers at the door, and the odd mixture of people suggests a Spain ready for drastic insurgency.

You won't see or feel such things unless you look for some time. A movie can spring from an image eager to bloom as much as from a storyline. Graham Greene said *The Third Man* started with a line he wrote on an envelope about the surprise of seeing a man on the street who had been buried just a week earlier. But I wonder if Carol Reed's film didn't believe in that night scene where noise brings a light in an upstairs window and it falls on the smile of Harry Lime (or Orson Welles), who also seemed to have been buried some time ago.

One viewing is enough, if one is all you get. In the 1980s I spoke to someone who had seen the long version of von Stroheim's *Greed,* in 1924—she couldn't remember it well (she had been seventeen), but she had thought it was amazing. (Stroheim's eight-hour version was eventually cut by the studio to just over two hours.) Think what a photograph of that screening would mean.

There is a speech in *Citizen Kane* by Bernstein. He is talking about the past and memory and he says he saw a girl once, in 1896, a woman in white with a white parasol, on the ferry over to Jersey. He never spoke to her or saw her again, but "I'll bet a month hasn't gone by since, that I haven't thought of that girl." It's a bittersweet moment, and Welles does not cut away to a glimpse of that woman (a Monet-like bloom) just to show you what Bernstein means. Not that *Citizen Kane* doesn't cut back and forth in time; but it's a movie in which there are only a few "nows," and all of them are ghosts from the past.

By 1955, I had been told about *Citizen Kane*; I had read of it in the few film books that existed then. But you couldn't see it: old films seldom came back. For all we knew they were lost. Then a local theater, the Classic in Tooting, announced it. I hurried there for the first screening, confident that there would be lines. I was the only member of the audience. This bewildered me so that I did not appreciate at first how providential that circumstance was.

Orson Welles was half-forgotten then. He had gone to Europe in a mood of disgrace or escape. *Kane* had had a working title of "American," but Welles was dismayed by his own country and what he saw as its abandonment of the FDR spirit. He may have had tax problems, and fears over investigation of his radical ties. He may have preferred Europe. But in the summer of 1955 he came to London for a flurry of activity: he married his third wife, Paola Mori, at Caxton Hall; and he appeared at the Duke of York's Theatre in a play he had made up out of Herman Melville, *Moby Dick Rehearsed*. It attracted attention and maybe someone said, "Well, suppose we showed

Citizen Kane again?" And suppose they found a magnificent print—for that is what I remember, a print direct from the negative, as if struck the day before.

I did not understand *Kane* when I saw it the first time, but I felt the shock of a film that was "difficult." The plot itself was beyond my grasp, I was not sure where to look and what to listen for in its dense texture. Most films, then and now, are signposted visually and aurally; everything is meant to be grasped on one viewing. *Kane* may have been the first American picture that required more than one viewing. I realized that the sled thrown into the furnace at the end was the source of "Rosebud" (at least, I think I did), but I was unsure how to feel the emotion or the irony in that resolution. One difficulty in keeping up with the film was the rapid shifts backward and forward in time, leaving so little "now" story. How can there be, when the hero, or whatever he is, dies in the first scene? Another difficulty was that this picture gave no help in knowing which people I should like, or not. This was especially relevant with Kane himself. He was charming, boyish, devil-may-care—but was he a devil, too? (A similar puzzle attends Harry Lime.) That matter of identification is still a problem in filmgoing: I have heard people say, Well, yes, Michael Haneke's *Amour* (2012) is all very fine, but truly that old man and woman are past our sympathy. They have given up being likeable, so they cannot stop life and death washing over them like a tide. Others say, But that's what elderly people are like and why *Amour* is so special.

I wanted to see *Kane* again, just as on your first visit to Madrid you wonder when you will get back to the Prado. You buy a postcard or a poster of *Las Meninas;* you keep looking. It is the same with a person—until you stop looking. If Bernstein had married that girl in white, he might not have remembered her so sharply.

A time came when I started seeing *Kane* regularly. I read the script and several books about Welles. This was going back to church and renewing one's vows, but I was getting more out of the picture all the time. It was in 1962, for the first time, that the film topped the *Sight & Sound* critics' poll. Yet it had not placed in the top ten in 1952, because many people had not seen it then. Where would you see it? How would you counter the notion that Welles was a burnt-out case? But by 1962, it was appreciated that Welles was still alive, still making films. *Touch of Evil* had opened in 1958, and it was not so much a comeback as a sardonic reappraisal of American film in the late fifties. In its deft, insolent way, it was about Mexican-American sexual threat, drugs, police corruption, and the rancid border. The burnt-out case was aflame, and still ahead of his time. In 1962, his film of Kafka's *The Trial*—with Anthony Perkins as Joseph K (or was it Norman K?), shot in the abandoned Gare d'Orsay—was unexpected, perversely inventive, and utterly European. Orson was giving immense interviews, and interview was his métier. He talked like a great traveler who had read everything and known every dancer. He was still younger than fifty. He made *Chimes at Midnight,* playing Falstaff. He was as far from burned-out as a ticking bomb.

Against the grain of the film's mounting eminence, Pauline Kael published her long essay, "Raising Kane," which sought to bring the picture down to size. She claimed it was a shallow masterpiece at a time when other writers were finding new depth in it. But Kael's point of view was contested by her own avowed habits. She was the leading American critic of that moment, and a very good writer. But she claimed she only ever saw a film once. The rationale for that was worth listening to. She said that movies were and ought to be sensational, immediate, and so compelling that one had to rely on the first viewing. If it didn't work straightaway, then it wasn't working. I sat next to her at a screening and she had a fierce intensity, hunched over her notebook, looking up at the screen and then at her notes in rapid succession—and the notes seemed to be fluent sentences, not just jottings for memory.

It was a disarming encounter, for plainly Kael was not always looking at the screen. If she really believed in nothing but the first time, how was she getting it all? Or was her mind being made up as she watched the film and by the process of writing? As I say, she was a picture of concentration, and an exciting writer whether or not one agreed with her. She coincided with a rich moment in the movies, and she made the medium seem important for her America. But was she to be trusted? Did she only ever see a film once? Was her regard for the shallowness of *Kane* valid if she had only paddled at its edges? Had she written her essay on just a single viewing?

Immediacy is vital, and for a long time the movies organized that adrenaline as suspense. So in *Intolerance* (1916), D. W. Griffith staged a race-against-time in its modern episode in which audiences were desperate to see whether a condemned man could be saved from execution. Years later, in *High Noon,* we were on tenterhooks to find out whether the lone figure of Gary Cooper's marshal could defeat the four murderous avengers who have come to his town to get him. Suspense of that kind was novel in 1916, and perhaps audiences were in true doubt over the outcome. But by 1952, movie had established its own system, so that we knew Coop was going to be all right. He might be wounded. He might need that new daughter-like wife (Grace Kelly) to come to his aid. But virtue would be rewarded—though it was striking and novel in 1952 when the heroic sheriff told his wretched town to look after itself, and he threw his star in the dust. (In *Touch of Evil*, the corrupt sheriff also turned in his badge.)

High Noon and *Intolerance* are made with great skill, and the people on view are appealing. Still, the more a film relies on pure suspense the less likely it is to hold an audience for long. A few years later, Cooper was the lead in another Western, *Man of the West*, in which he is a reformed outlaw caught up in the deadly moods of his own past. In 1957, you could assume that Coop would survive that test, but *Man of the West* is more complicated than survival can handle. Suspense has yielded to a tragic understanding of the West. By 1971 it was far less clear that McCabe would survive in *McCabe & Mrs Miller*. Could he kill off the bad guys the way Coop did? I won't answer that question, in case you haven't seen the film. But it is waiting for you, and it leads the picture into a mood of fatalism, not triumph. You'll have to see it again, as soon as you've seen it once, just to try to hear what is said and see everything that happens. Its director, Robert Altman, was a pioneer in not making things clear—and clarity is death if you like to see films again and again. But the idea of unclarity in movie was a heresy, or even the end of cinema as fun. John Wayne, that rock of the Western genre, disapproved of these anti-heroic films and thought they signaled a decline in American manliness.

I don't want to see *The Usual Suspects* again now that I know who Keyser Söze is. Instead, I see that movie as a mass of mannered implausibilities, and witty character acting, that bets all its chips on the thing we don't know. The eventual revelation destroys the film's fragile mood. I think I know from the established tropes of movies that by the end of *The Godfather* and *The Godfather Part II* Michael Corleone is going to be secure in his power. But I can't forget the tension in those two films between the dead end of power and the liveliness of all the characters, and I believe that it becomes not just a Mafia movie, but a stricken study in how attractive gangsters and their sleek elegance can be. I have thought over the years that there might be an even greater film in the two *Godfather*s if Kay (Diane Keaton), the least explored character, becomes so horrified by Michael that she goes to the law and becomes a witness against him. But we hardly notice that the cops barely figure in these films. *The Sopranos* was similarly short of lawmen. Crime has become so organized on our screens, so tranquil, it is not to be interfered with.

In the early history of gangster films, or crime movies, there was never room for doubt. In the thirties and forties, every code required that crime could not pay, except at the box office. From *Public Enemy* to *White Heat,* Cagney ran amok—to our delight. His liberty was permitted because we knew he would be destroyed finally—and because the system making the film knew we knew. So if you get into the habit of watching *White Heat* again and again, I think you're reveling in the fantasy of violence. That may be how you begin to forget the damage it causes.

Throughout the 1970s, I taught film and steadily offered *Citizen Kane* to American students, some of whom still regarded Welles as an overweight bon vivant who did cynical ads for cheap wines. A teacher tends to preach a film; in which case his mind is made up. When you are strong in erasing other people's doubts, you neglect your own. At Dartmouth, I taught a seminar on Welles, until in the early eighties I realized I was not looking at the film any longer. I knew what to say about it, and that stopped me thinking. Perhaps that happened on a wider scale. *Kane* topped that *Sight & Sound* poll from 1962 to 2002, and the film was taken for granted. It became axiomatic, and that gave up the shock and excitement—the sensation— that I had felt in Tooting. Welles himself (he only died in 1985) said he could no longer look at his picture, and I followed suit with six or seven years of moratorium. I came back, and the film was alive again, but to this day I know that afternoon in Tooting was the crucial occasion.

In a university, a film teacher might exchange common room gossip with people teaching Dickens, Mozart, and Velázquez. They were charmed to hear you were doing *Citizen Kane,* but *The Flame and the Arrow?* I choose that 1950 movie almost at random because at the age of nine I loved the thrill of imagining myself as Burt Lancaster, with Virginia Mayo as my prize, in a never-never land called Lombardy in the twelfth century. I saw the film a couple of times in 1950 and I reveled in Burt's grin, his cheek, and his backflips. "Lombardy" looked magical in Technicolor. So it needed to be, for the film was shot on a ranch in California's Simi Valley. The picture was enriched by several supporting players: Nick Cravat (Burt's regular side-kick), Robert Douglas, and Norman Lloyd. It was a Warner Bros. picture and I trusted that studio and its blithe sense of history. The film was in color, photographed by Ernest Haller, with music by Max Steiner. Both men had done *Gone With the Wind.* It was directed by Jacques Tourneur, and Waldo Salt had written the script.

Later on, the film scholar would discover that Waldo Salt had been blacklisted. He had joined the Communist Party in 1938. He was vital to Joseph Losey's superb remaking of *M.* But later on he would write *Midnight Cowboy* and *Coming Home.* So maybe the story of peasants revolting against cruel lords in old Lombardy was a political metaphor? Tourneur was a director with great visual aplomb: he had done *Out of the Past* just a few years earlier, and that is still a classic noir with Robert Mitchum and Jane Greer.

Still, *The Flame and the Arrow* was routine fare, and a big hit: it had domestic rentals of $3 million. It was ideal for a nine-year-old in 1950, and something some six-year-olds would enjoy now. But truly you could have too much of it, or take it too seriously. You wouldn't worry that most of the pleasure and the sensation of the film was there now, immediately, the first time you saw it—perhaps 90 percent? Here was a film like thousands of others meant to fill around ninety minutes with delight, and which was based on the principle that in three days' time there would be something else on your screen just as entertaining.

Could it be studied—*should* it be? Was there a Marxist subtext and Ph.D. prospects in *The Flame and the Arrow*? Had this movie threatened American military cohesion in the year the Korean War began? (It was released two weeks after the Korean People's Army crossed the 38th parallel.) Or was there another subtext that it took me fifty years to discover? Was the movie begging for the kind of affectionate parody of Hollywood movies provided by Carol Burnett or Monty Python? And once you were alert to parody, what was this about two chums, Dardo and Piccolo, hiding out in the forest and sniping at tyranny? Their acrobatics and their insouciant smiles were a kind of schoolboy ballet. How did forest dwellers stay so buffed and trim? How were their teeth perfect? (Their smiles were as important as any love of nature, archery, or Anne of

Hesse. Virginia Mayo's promotion: from her days in St. Louis and vaudeville, she was known as the pin-up who had come to life.) Was there a suggestion of gay brotherhood in Burt and Nick Cravat? The two actors had been boyhood friends; they joined the circus together; and then went to Hollywood. Both of them were married with children, but there is a legend now that Lancaster was gay, too. Why not?

There were more far-reaching films made in 1950, like *Sunset Blvd., All About Eve,* or Max Ophüls's *La Ronde,* which was regarded as a "naughty" film not fit for children. Was it "naughty" to expose anyone to an ironic, dispassionate survey of love as a human infection? Whereas *The Flame and the Arrow* in Britain had a U certificate (open to any age) and I actually went to see it on my own. In those times, I tried whatever was on—like the bulk of the filmgoing audience. Sometimes I knew no more than a title, a poster, and an actor's name. What I really went for were the ninety minutes of escape, the fun, the sensation, the silly nowness of it all.

That attitude meant a film could never match that first impact when it came up on the screen like this morning's sun, and innocence could ask, "Will Dardo win?" There are still good, pleasing films that deserve no more than a single viewing—I hope this doesn't shock you but I'd put *The Artist, Slumdog Millionaire, Million Dollar Baby, The King's Speech,* and *Gravity* in that category. Some of them won Best Picture at the Oscars, but once was enough. They are smart, confident entertainments, nicely played, but they have no significant ambition or sense of mystery. They are small stories, well told, and all deeply old-fashioned, even when the effects are very special. The most intriguing thing about *The King's Speech* is that it could have been made in 1937 at a time when a speech defect could seem, to the king, the gravest issue in the world.

Try those films again: a boredom may begin to arise with the reiteration of so much niceness. For decades I watched *Citizen Kane* and believed I was getting more out of it: the possibility that the whole film was a daydream in Kane's head as he died; the ironic place of applause; the rueful examination of the dangers in charm; the fallibility of memory. There were plenty of other movies as rich—Buñuel's *Un Chien Andalou,* Renoir's *La Règle du Jeu,* most of Bresson and Ophüls, Resnais's *Hiroshima Mon Amour,* several films by Kenji Mizoguchi, Ingmar Bergman's *Persona* and *Cries and Whispers,* Godard's *Pierrot le Fou*—or, more recently, *Blue Velvet* and *Mulholland Dr.* by David Lynch, *No Country for Old Men* by the Coen brothers, *Magnolia* by Paul Thomas Anderson, David Fincher's *Zodiac,* or Martin Scorsese's *Casino.*

When I first saw *Casino,* in 1995, I didn't like it. I regarded it as yet one more Scorsese gangster film, monopolized by its own violence and the inflammatory and implausible eloquence of hoodlums, with jukebox accompaniment and the dazzle of Las Vegas. Scorsese is vulnerable on all those counts, and on his reluctance in developing female characters. But ten years or so after *Casino* opened theatrically, the film played regularly on cable TV stations. I found myself watching it repeatedly (although I still reckoned I didn't like it). What was happening? Well, in part it was the sheer cinematic fluency of the picture and its relaxed attitude to plot. Ostensibly, it concerned the rivalry between two friends (Robert De Niro and Joe Pesci) and how that turmoil ruined the sweet money mine of Las Vegas for both of them. Hadn't that game been played in *Goodfellas,* and even in *Raging Bull?* But in *Casino,* there was a variation: De Niro was the rational, orderly man fit to make the system work, while Pesci was madness determined to fuck it up. (It's order and chaos, just like in *Locke.*) That was

more interesting than the male relationships in Scorsese's earlier films, because it began to offer (or I began to see) De Niro's
character, "Ace" Rothstein, as a tragic fool.

What I never saw at first—and I'm not sure it was intended
by the filmmakers—was the desperate comedy of De Niro
being thwarted at every turn. This added to the disaster of his
marriage to Ginger (Sharon Stone), the fullest female character
in Scorsese's work. She is greedy, treacherous, self-destructive, a
thief, and a slut, but she fascinates Scorsese as much as she does
"Ace." So *Casino* is a story about a failed marriage, full of pain,
but unable to shake off the tinge of gallows humor.

Does this mean that if you watch any film long enough it
gets better? Alas, no; there are plenty of films that discourage
you (or me) from trying again. I'm not going back to Lars von
Trier's *Melancholia* or Terrence Malick's *The Tree of Life*. If you
admire those films, we must live with our disagreements. It's
not as if there is any true state of being right or wrong. In suggesting "how to watch a movie," I do not intend to present you
with a tidy pantheon or a set of correct answers.

Earlier, I mentioned the rumor that old people say movies
can shift over time. But they can't change, can they, not in a
medium reliant on mechanical reproduction? Well, sad things
do happen: almost any color system except Technicolor tends
to deteriorate; it's not common these days to see films projected
(or shown on television) in the Academy frame format that was
intended. You wouldn't respect *Las Meninas* as much if thick
strips top and bottom had been removed from it. Some studios
neglect their own treasures, so the negatives of great films suffer and will never be what they were. By now, it is increasingly
difficult to find prints of films you love—they come as digital
projection packages. And the two things are not the same, even

if the digital formats are more economical and convenient. The one was made from light, the other comes from electronics. So far at least, digital has been a little less human, a trait exacerbated by its facility at showing things that never could have happened.

Then there is the matter of how movies date, sometimes over years, but sometimes over the weekend. When *The Exorcist* opened in 1973 it was a very frightening experience. I had no faith in the devil or being possessed, but the growling voice coming out of the child's head gave me the shivers. The film was a box-office hit. But when it was re-released in 2000, the tension was gone. People in the audience were laughing at it and at the idea that once upon a time they or their parents had been terrified. We take rapid vengeance on things that have frightened us.

So movies can shift. Of course, for its golden years, the film business never envisaged or cared about that alteration. They took the money in their now, the thing we regard as then. I had to wait a while to learn the emotional wisdom in some Lubitsch films—*Trouble in Paradise, The Shop Around the Corner, To Be or Not to Be.* A similar passage of time was necessary to see that Howard Hawks's comedies were richer than the epic companionship of *Red River* or *Air Force* or *The Big Sky.* Hadn't I always realized that *Rio Bravo, To Have and Have Not,* and *The Big Sleep,* despite the apparent crises of guarding a prisoner, saving Resistance fighters, and finding a killer, were comedies made by a man who had little respect for murder, war, or law and order, and no interest in anything except flight, women, and dreaming?

We should be wary of ourselves and that first viewing, no matter how heady it was at the time. When they opened in

London, I saw *Bonnie and Clyde* and *Pierrot le Fou* five times in a week. Those films had a visceral, sensational rush, akin to the hot water in a shower or the taste of salted caramel ice cream. It's like your first encounter with serious kissing, and classical cinema adored the kiss. You want to do it again and again, and maybe those first kisses are the most momentous.

My love of film says, Again, please; and DVD lets me look at some highlight instead of the full, tedious ninety minutes: Fred Astaire and Eleanor Powell dancing "Begin the Beguine" over and over so I don't have to bother with the rest of *Broadway Melody of 1940*—I can now no longer remember what happens in that story. (George Murphy is the other man in that film, and he is as unnoticed now as a man who might have been with the woman in white on Bernstein's ferry to Jersey. Murphy was also the U.S. senior senator from California from 1965 to 1971—I suppose someone had to be.)

So I saw *The Big Sleep* three times one Saturday during the first Hawks season at the London National Film Theatre. I didn't care about the plot—and it's a matter of famous history that Hawks didn't either. But I treasured being there with it and longing to be up on the screen in General Sternwood's hothouse, at the Acme book store as it closed for the afternoon, and in the car (or the shell of a car on a soundstage), where Bogart and Bacall gave up on snarly wisecracks at each other. They tried a kiss and went on from there.

5

WATCHING AND SEEING

Keep your eyes peeled!" I was told as a child—it might be for unexploded bombs, Nazi spies, or sixpence on the street. I relished the advice and I have tried to live by it, and sometimes these days you have to be alert lest someone locked into their iPhone (one of the new body-snatched?) bumps into you. It *is* worth looking.

"Attention must be paid!" is the plaintive urging from Arthur Miller's play *Death of a Salesman* (1949), and what it calls for is our looking closely at this man Willy Loman, not simply for his own sake, but because he is a metaphor for changed times, and because not being noticed was already perceived as a threat of larger cultural invisibility. Willy's wife, Linda, tells their children: "I don't say he's a great man. Willy Loman never made a lot of money. His name was never in the paper. He's not the finest character that ever lived. But he's a human being, and a terrible thing is happening to him. So attention must be paid. He's not to be allowed to fall in his grave like an old dog."

He is not just Willy Loman, he is a dying salesman in an economy where that plight will become salutary. Loman is as old-fashioned as Bob Cratchit; he was door-to-door and selling is instant actual. Even if you've never seen *Death of a Salesman,* you likely get it from what I've told you. The play is a moral-social-literary tract that simply waits to be illustrated onstage—and I believe it's an overrated classic. But his wife has this sense of attention as a kind of moral duty: Did you really *look* at Loman? What color were his suit and his hat, his shirt and his tie? If you were directing it anew onstage, what wardrobe decisions would you make? Did Willy seem to walk OK or could you tell his feet were folding under him from carrying suitcases of samples up hopeless staircases? Look at his eyes. Oh, you can't quite see the eyes in the theater? Very well, perhaps we need a new medium, one that can break your heart with eyes and their sadness. In which case we'll need an actor who can do sad-eye. Dustin Hoffman?—too old. Lee J. Cobb?—dead. Brian Dennehy?—too robust. Philip Seymour Hoffman?—he played the role onstage not long before he died. Don't worry—the applications are lining up. Star actors are coming to audition, down-at-heel and melancholy. It's actors' sad-eye that has pumped pathos into attention.

In a book called *How to Watch a Movie,* do you really need this instruction in keeping your eyes open? We'll see.

As I write, I have just come back from walking my dog in the early morning at Crissy Fields in San Francisco. That is an expanse of meadow and shore that looks out to the water, the Pacific, Alcatraz Island, and the Golden Gate Bridge. It is a walk I have done a few thousand times. Today, as on every day, I looked at the bridge with a facet of its brick color made amber or gold or pink (whatever) in the rising sun. I surveyed the water and the small waves coming in. I noticed some people I usually see on these walks, and I watched the dog. I also noticed the geese feeding on the grass; they are often there, fifty or so of the gray-black birds. I did look to see if the heron was there—he or she often is—but not today. I didn't see a coyote, but that slinky shape is there sometimes at dawn.

I looked at the bridge but I saw nothing—no collapse in its structure; no vehicle on fire; no one jumping off into the water. I looked at Fort Point, the tip of land beneath the southern end of the bridge, but I saw no hint of a blonde woman in a gray suit plunging into the water. So I didn't have to consider diving in after her, and that's a mercy if you have vertigo. When I got home, my wife asked, "Did you have a nice walk?" I said it had been grand. "What happened?" she asked. "Oh, nothing," I replied.

A camera is helplessly open, yet it doesn't see things. We live in an age now of surveillance footage where a camera in a top corner of some location records any transgression against the emptiness of that space. (Do you remember Nina, the revealed betrayer, looking up at the surveillance in the last episode of the first series of 24?) If you imagine the hapless observer who has to study hours and years of that footage, you know seeing could be soporific—until a stray coyote or a terrorist sidles through the space. You set up a camera, you adjust its lens, its focus, and its exposure (these are antique habits now) and it will "take" whatever is in front of it. We still trust that documentary fidelity, even though we know it is easy for the cinematic system to manufacture imagery that has no provenance or authenticity and insert it in the space.

But human beings don't watch in the way of a camera. Go to the door, or the street, or the beach and try taking in the totality of what there is to be seen. You can't do it, for our attention notices particular things: the coyote, or the white goose. If that pretty girl (whatever pretty is) walks by, you notice her, you look at her, you focus on her, and you pan with her walk. You hope you're seeing her (as in looking into her) and you would not mind if she noticed that. For you would like to earn her attention. If attention has to be paid, it is encouraged by being noticed. "That guy was looking at me again today," she may tell a friend. To which the friend replies, in a take-it-or-leave-it way, "Maybe he fancies you."

Then there's a look on the girl's face that's so hard to describe—hopeful, dubious, wistful, ready—so we're going to need an actress. You can say to the actress, Well, tomorrow, when we do that scene, how would you play it? She may reply, You're the director, what do you want me to do? And in intriguing ways, this discussion is what a real girl might puzzle over while deciding whether she should look up at the watcher and give the hint of a smile, a germ of recognition, or of being noticed?

Any work that involves a camera must have the animating impetus of someone who watches and wants to see. In Alfred Hitchcock's *Rear Window* (1954) James Stewart plays a photojournalist, L. B. Jeffries, confined to his New York apartment because of a broken leg. He was injured taking one of the dangerous pictures for which he is famous. But now he is idle, bored, doing nothing except entertaining his girlfriend, Lisa (Grace Kelly); resist her suggestions about their getting married or have a massage administered by the dry, tart Stella (Thelma Ritter). What would you do?

Well, you might read a lot of books or listen to music or watch television (this was 1954—he could have seen the Army–McCarthy hearings, that crucial step in Joe McCarthy's downfall), but movies in the 1950s felt it was tasteless to show a TV. So Jeff starts to look out of his window at the courtyard and the several apartments that are visible. He is a casual snoop, an everyday voyeur, just a laid-up cameraman, restless and amused by the lives he sees. He has a carefree narcissism in that, while staring at these strangers, he never realizes they can see him.

None of these people sharing the courtyard are his friends. But then his nearly vacant survey notices something—like that man in the doorway in *Las Meninas*. In one apartment opposite him, a man and his wife are always arguing—this is enough to convince Jeff not to get married. But then the wife is no longer there and the husband is behaving suspiciously. The photographer starts to watch or keep watch. He doesn't go to bed but stays in his chair in the dark, drifting off to sleep then waking—is he dreaming? Or has his empty-headed looking turned into a vigil so that now he sees enough to make him think the white-haired man across the way (his name is Lars Thorwald) has murdered his wife?

His policeman friend (Wendell Corey) mocks Jeff's theory, but it turns out to be right. As I said, this is a movie made in 1954 by Alfred Hitchcock, and nothing to complain about. Its great entertainment is also a study in watching that teaches us to look closely and that exploits our urge to see. But the spectacle has been set up with seeing in mind, so the factual strand is overlaid with fictional intent. The Thorwalds fit Jeff's imagination. Mrs. Thorwald (Irene Winston) is harsh-voiced, with red-ginger hair and strained features. She is so far from the loveliness of girlfriend Grace Kelly. And Thorwald (Raymond Burr) is a trapped bear of a man; he feels too bulky for his apartment. He seems powerful, despite his noticeable white hair—and Raymond Burr had dark hair. In other words, the Thorwalds have been cast and dressed to fit Jeff's bill.

And while Hitchcock, more than most directors, is obsessed with particular pointed seeing, he organizes the seen thing to the point of claustrophobia. We are not in a real Manhattan courtyard, where fickle weather, stray birds, and unexpected and irrelevant incidents may occur. We are looking at an elaborate set (built in Los Angeles) where fate has been taken in hand. When Grace Kelly does something brave (like going over to the Thorwald apartment when it is empty to search for the wife's wedding ring), there is a shot of Jeff looking at her in which we realize he sees her in a new light. She isn't simply an empty-headed beauty. She has the right stuff. He will marry her—even if some husbands kill their wives. (Actually, the panorama of the courtyard presents several different aspects of marriage: the honeymooners behind drawn blinds; the sexpot dancer who has many gentleman callers while her husband is in the military; the elderly couple who exist in terms of their dog; two lonely people who long for companionship; the Thorwalds; and Jeff himself, happy enough to have Lisa stay the night but reluctant to be tied down.)

Even in 1954, the courtyard in *Rear Window* never felt like an actual place. Hitchcock built it for convenience and to facilitate shooting as the plan of a place. That's how "décor" is a distillation of meaning or a caption, as well as a location. Hitch was not impressed by realism, or always mindful of it. All his life he used back projections when even an untrained audience could see and feel that artifice. He didn't care. He chose every item that we would see, arranged and composed them like parts of a theorem because he worked on the principle that everything we could see we would interpret. We are like Jeffries in that way: we see costume, hairstyle, or a way of walking, and we start to read those things into some pattern or meaning. Most movies partake of that logic in a relentless way that is sometimes the opposite of documentary liberty. The whole thing, the view, is a setup.

And yet, there are moments even in *Rear Window* when documentary presence breaks through. When Lisa hunts for that ring, and when Thorwald starts to return, the suspense is based on the spatial reality, the way we see Thorwald and Lisa in the same apartment, with her life under threat. When Lisa flutters her hands behind her back to show Jeff—she knows he is watching—the ring she had found and put on her own finger, there is an insouciance, a cockiness, an impudent grace about the way she does it that is just Kelly; it's what we love about her. Now, Hitch was directing her, and he might have directed her more closely. But if you recast Lisa with Kim Novak (another Hitchcock actress of that moment), I think the gesture would be more awkward, more shy, more afraid, maybe. This is speculation, but it is a way of suggesting how many unique, natural things there can be—pieces of documentary, if you like—in any contrived and controlled movie.

But the moment Lisa has waggled her fingers, freedom is brushed aside by willful selection. For Thorwald notices the gesture, and traces the line of sight back to the apartment where Jeff is watching. He gazes into the film's camera with an unforgettable mixture of reproach and malice. It is the first time anyone in the courtyard has noticed Jeff—or us. So

Thorwald at last knows who has been spying on him and tormenting him, and who may bring him to justice.

Thorwald works his way through the building, searching for Jeff's apartment. We are as afraid as Jeff; we fear the worst. And that's where Hitch pulls a clever trick. The trapped beast in Thorwald opens the door, looks into the dark, and asks, "What do you want of me?" He is menacing, but he is pathetic. His question is unexpected, and it's fair to hear it as Hitch asking the voyeurs in the audience, Well, what *do* you expect of this wretched man? What obligation does the voyeur have to the thing spied on? Hitch barely hesitates over this question. He hurries into the climax and the contrived business of Jeff holding Thorwald at bay with exploding flash bulbs. But there, sixty years ago, the question was raised, and it means more now—why are we watching and what do we think we see? More than that: do we give the thing being seen a chance?

Now, I am not suggesting that Thorwald in *Rear Window* deserves to be excused or pardoned, just because he had a shrewish wife and a nagging spy on his trail. But consider watching or questioning in a larger context. In 1954, more or less, Americans were told that when they looked at Soviet Russia they saw an enemy; when they looked at Communism they easily imagined Reds under the bed or the threat of infiltrating power able to possess their own nuclear weapons; when they looked at Indochina (as it was known then) wasn't there the potential for a domino theory of Communist influence in southeast Asia? The most powerful and prosperous country in the world, the United States, was being warned to feel edgy or insecure—no matter that the Soviet Union and nationalist movements in Indochina had so much more to be afraid of. Communism means next to nothing now as a present danger. But our public discourse, our watching, which had lately acquired television as a new way of seeing, was loaded then with messages and anxiety, so that the things being seen had little liberty to ask, Can't you see us for what we are? What dominating threats will be as faded away fifty years from now as Communism?

Today, the means of survey have become so much more thorough and expensive. We are realizing that our own state is so nervous it is inclined to watch us, too, and not just other nations. When watching is allied to technology, it knows very few restraints. So the pressure on "seeing," as in trying to understand, becomes greater and far harder to sustain.

What do we really know about Iran and North Korea, except that they are "enemies"? This line of thought may seem remote from watching movies, but it's not, because the world is now screened for us in so many ways. And yet the questing dynamic of *Rear Window* ("I don't think I like what I'm seeing") assists the very loaded partiality of how we are seeing. Judicious observation means watching with as little bias as possible. It deserves a far more extensive, objective news system than we have—and that limitation owes more to economy and ideology than to technology. Such a service might recall that Ho Chi Minh, Saddam Hussein, and Osama bin Laden were our allies before they were our enemies. Perhaps that posture made them cunning opportunists, but much of the world judges us now in exactly those terms.

To put the matter at what may be the most testing level of all, what did the inspection process of films of the 1950s see in women? And how did it fit with the new ideas of feminism? Well, Marilyn Monroe, Elizabeth Taylor, Grace Kelly, Audrey Hepburn, and many others may have been adored creatures in the fifties and into the sixties, but they were also instruments in male fantasies. Grace Kelly's character in *Rear Window*—Lisa Carol Fremont—has many cinematic assets: she is attractive, smart, brave, funny, and obedient. At the end of the movie, she is still "with" the Jimmy Stewart photographer, waiting for him to recover and return to his career of photography. They don't seem to be married.

It was part of this business in the 1950s, and still to this day, that men will pay to look at pretty women in attractive sexual situations, and in stories where being a woman seldom threatens the way men think of the world and their authority. I'm not just talking about degrees of physical nakedness and allure—though much more is still expected of actresses than actors in that respect. More significantly, it's a matter of whether women's thinking penetrates the nature of our stories. Yes, there are changes to be welcomed: films like John Cassavetes's *A Woman Under the Influence,* where the director's wife (Gena Rowlands) played a woman who was breaking down and making life "impossible" for her husband, or *Klute,* where Jane Fonda's "sexy" hooker could make a male viewer sheepish over the way that role is generally depicted. We have outstanding women directors now, but not too many—the achievement of Jane Campion (*The Piano, Top of the Lake*), Kathryn Bigelow (*The Hurt Locker, Zero Dark Thirty*), Claire Denis (*Beau Travail, White Material*), and Lynne Ramsay (*Ratcatcher, Morvern Callar*) is one of talent and persistence, but I may already be into names you don't know. The astonishing eminence and talent of Leni Riefenstahl in Germany in the 1930s should not be excluded because of her ideology (*Triumph of the Will, Olympia*). And women are still not welcomed as cinematographers, which speaks to a nearly occult fear of women doing the crucial, secret "looking." (Women make up 2 percent of American cinematographers.)

For every step taken toward gender liberation, the Internet has unleashed a craze for wardrobe malfunctions, boobs and butts "we" love, and archaic but intrusive pinup galleries from a dark, depressing age. Our commercials still employ iconography, attitudes, and models that sustain a mythology of sexual attractiveness or beauty being vital to our lifeblood of purchase.

We have never been happy with this state of affairs, and by the 1960s some movies had grasped that as a subject. In Michelangelo Antonioni's *Blow-Up* (1966), Thomas (David Hemmings) is a fashionable London photographer and a chronically alienated young man. He is a lord of what he surveys, a director of scenes. He can command a troupe of beautiful, numb female models to pose at his will, and he prompts one of these women into having sex, not quite with him, but with his camera. Equally, he can turn shabby and homeless and arrive in the evening at a doss house, his expensive camera wrapped in old newspaper, so that he can photograph tramps and derelicts. It is a part of his insolence that he has beauty and wretchedness on the same roll, and he is paid by Sunday magazines that will run the two types of photograph side-by-side, as confessional boasts of our contradictory culture.

But Thomas is untouched: he is not sexually aroused by the models; he has no compassion for the tramps. He may be aspiring to Christopher Isherwood's famous declaration "I am a camera," because that mechanical neutrality might offer a way of passing through life without being hurt, involved, or responsible.

One day, Thomas finds himself in a park in southeast London. Despite the pleasant summer day, the place seems nearly empty, except for a man and a woman in the distance who might be lovers. It's hard to tell. Thomas is intrigued, and from a safe distance, with his telephoto lens, he photographs the couple. He isolates them from the park and the surround of reality and wonders if they have a story. Though Antonioni treats the park with cool detachment, we feel the space and the greenery, we see the trees toss in the wind, and we hear the tiny sounds of nature. But Thomas picks his couple as subjects or characters. He has decided they are "photogenic" without really thinking why.

The woman in the couple (Vanessa Redgrave) sees what Thomas is doing and hurries toward him in anger and distress. She demands that he give her the roll of film, but Thomas's coldness grows with her alarm and the claim that he has invaded her privacy. He teases her into a later meeting where she offers him her body in exchange for the film. But sex means less to Thomas than film. He tricks her, sends her away, and prepares to develop the precious roll.

What follows is one of the most beautiful and intense sequences in film. It describes inanimate objects and a technical process, but it is as beguiling as watching Garbo being alone or Bogart strolling across a room. The identification, the being there, amounts to a rapture. Working in the darkroom, Thomas brings his negatives to life and begins to see not just a series of frames in time but the possibility of a story. A sensation! He makes enlargements of detail. He pins the pictures on the wall, in order, like a storyboard. And he comes to believe that the man who was with Redgrave may have been murdered. In the park, Thomas didn't notice this happen, but his camera may have taken it in and kept the information for his discovery.

You should pursue *Blow-Up* to see what happens next, but I can tell you the resolution is uncertain, as if it carries some suggestion that you can hardly trust photography, let alone what you think you see. There are so many fallacious clichés about film and photography—"A picture is worth a thousand words" and "Cinema is truth twenty-four times per second"—in that film seems to have a blunt, down-to-earth pact with reality that no verbal description can possess or surpass.

But is that so, or reliable? The claim that a picture is worth a thousand words does match the sensation we have all felt on seeing something startling beyond belief—the approach of a tsunami, Bob Beamon long-jumping 29 feet 2½ inches in Mexico City on October 18, 1968, an accelerated movie of clouds rushing across the sky to escape night, or pictures from a concentration camp. In 1943, a Polish Resistance fighter, Witold Pilecki, deliberately had himself imprisoned in Auschwitz to establish the facts about the camp. He made a hundred-page report, with photographs. He then escaped from the camp and carried the report to the Allies, but they deemed that it was exaggerated or unreliable. Then in 1945, the film director George Stevens shot 16 mm footage at the liberation of Dachau and it was later made into a documetary shown in the course of the Nuremberg Trials.

Watching and seeing are both physical (optical) and emotional (irrational). In its first sixty or so years, movie had made us all more conscious of looking: it had invested appearance with a new excitement, glamour, and erotic force. That energy is still there, but is it wearing off? This is the dilemma of the Internet—of so much to see that attention wavers or loses faith in itself. There has been a similarly jaded response to filmed stories. How often a picture begins and in just a few moments we are saying, Oh yes, I know this one . . . Instead of rapt spectators of the lifelike, we have become like screenwriters or editors.

A novelty in *Blow-Up* is that a moment comes when it assesses its own suspense plot and blows it away, like the petals on a dry flower. Thomas may think of himself as a brave young detective, like L. B. Jeffries in *Rear Window*. But Antonioni is not naive enough to credit that myth. He lets us see, yes, the body was there on screen, but then it vanishes. It may be an infernal conspiracy, in which case the wrongdoers go free (like Gavin Elster, the villain in Hitchcock's *Vertigo*). Or perhaps it was all a dream, or even a mocking satire on "reality," so that Thomas will end up playing tennis with a mime, chasing a nonexistent ball (even if the sound track starts to give us the happy "thock" of racket on ball). *Blow-Up* feints to be a mystery and concludes as a comedy in which the greatest fun comes from our childish urge to get everything sorted out.

Here is a vital point in watching a movie, or watching anything. It is heavenly to see your baby sleeping. We do it for hours on end, and then we pause and sleep because there will be tomorrow and tomorrow and maybe fifty years of it in which loving attention will hardly notice the child growing older. Or you can look at your baby and be so eager that you want to know its whole life story now—you want happiness settled and doubt expunged. I am going to suggest that as a model for watching movies and a way of fighting through their cunning diversions of story and plot while insisting on the continuity of looking. For decades, movies believed they should settle everything: some characters were dead, some were alive; these were happy, those were not. So we could go home with a tidy experience.

But this has gone on long enough now for us to become more intelligent, or to sink into the uncertainty that is inherent in watching and filming. The best mysteries are unsettled, even if that appeals to fewer people than those delighted by Sherlock Holmes's triumphant answers. Just before *Blow-Up*, in Italy, Antonioni had made an extraordinary film, *L'Eclisse*. It is about two lovers—played by Monica Vitti and Alain Delon. They are no better suited as a couple than are those two actors (though there is some chemistry). But we wonder what will become of their relationship—so many films hang on that issue. They make an arrangement to meet, and the film ends at the intersection they had agreed on. It is late afternoon, and life goes by in a multitude of ways. But the lovers do not appear. What does this mean?

So many fine, entertaining films say, *That's* what it means!—I can think of *Casablanca, Double Indemnity, Red River, The Big Heat, The Usual Suspects* (in its sneaky way), *The King's Speech* . . . so many of them—and I don't seek to diminish those works or their confident conclusions. But an evolving cinema and the loss of its automatic audience has led us more and more toward, *What* does this mean?, and that question requires us to carry on watching. Any film has to end, for conventional, businesslike reasons, but surely its mystery lives on in our heads. Isn't it remarkable that conclusions to *The Sopranos, The Wire,* and *True Detective* manage to be so open-ended that we regret having no more?

Think of David Cronenberg's *A History of Violence* (2005). The very title warns us of far-reaching concerns; forty years ago such a story might have been called *Return of the Past,* or *Desperate.* The hero, Tom (Viggo Mortensen), would have been driven from his quiet provincial life and his settled family back to the big bad city and the life of crime that made him. *Out of the Past* (1947) has a similar structure. So Tom kills his crime boss brother, Richie (William Hurt). Whereupon, as the film ends, you can wonder if he returns to the hinterland—or does he take power in the crime family he has sought to deny? That question hangs open—it's usually the films we've had enough of already that get sequels, never things as pregnant as *The History of Violence*.

I'll end this discussion with an example of close attention, while suggesting that the most daring novelty in *Citizen Kane* was not its deep-focus photography, overlapping sound, or flashback structure (though those things are truly difficult). The greater challenge was in saying, Don't expect one viewing to settle this—or even several. For the mystery here is the most precious thing. Unknowability is close to where this film is leading. For 1941, that was not just daring or innovative; it was close to a denial of the entertainment medium.

So at the start of *Kane,* after the nocturnal shots of Xanadu, where Kane lives—the menageries at night, the artworks, and the "No Trespassing" sign—the movie cuts to a large close-up of lips, with a mustache above them. The mouth says, "Rosebud"; the whisper is grandiose and trembling with echoes. We see a glass ball in a man's hand containing a small house and the effect of snow. This ball slips to the floor and shatters. Through a shard of that glass we see the warped door to a room open and a nurse, a woman in white, comes in.

Welles makes our looking, or our attention, as tricky as possible. He was always inclined to conceal secrets. We never see the room in what is called a master shot, sufficient to convey basic information. Yet the implication is that the man saying "Rosebud," the great mouth, and the glass ball are part of the same space and action. The shots are short and mannered; the black-and-white filming is very dramatic. The sight of the nurse is distorted by the broken glass. Amid this heightened looking, some people do not quite see or realize the way "Rosebud" is uttered *before* the nurse enters the room.

You can argue that she heard the word from outside the door, or that there was someone else inside the room who'd heard it and told her. But we are not shown those things, and that which is not shown hardly exists. Every movie is not just a story, or a mystery, it is an information system in which things are revealed to us as the film thinks fit. Welles could have shot the death of Charles Foster Kane—this is what we are talking about—in a conventional master shot where we see Kane in his last chair. We might gather how he dies. He might have company or attendants. We could hear the word and see the ball slip from his lifeless hand. Then the nurse steps forward. That would make it clear, or clearer. But it is essential to this great film that Welles wants the moment vivid, but mysterious, unsettling and fascinating. It's up to us. In other words, he has invited the spectator to a part of his film as it begins. He's telling a story but he wants us to remember he's building a film, too, in which we must be active.

After all, at the end of the film the printed word "Rosebud" will be picked up by an unwitting worker—it is the painted name on a boy's old sled—and tossed into the furnace. Then the camera will close in, the music will rise to an anguished but exhilarated emotional peak, and we will see the scroll lettering of "Rosebud," but only for a few seconds before the word melts away in the heat.

Do you see the affinity with the opening of a movie that is organized as a question, What does Rosebud mean? Just as no character in the film is seen to have heard the last word, so none of the searchers discovers this possible answer to what it signifies. Except for us, alone and together. Does it help to know that Orson Welles all his life loved conjuring and magic? Do you begin to grasp how fully you must watch if you hope to see?

6

WHAT IS CINEMATIC INFORMATION?

A French surveillance film inspector once studied five thousand hours of a mysteriously neglected parking lot on the outskirts of a city. He was attentive to the same fixed frame, and he reported on how few cars parked there and of how the drivers were hunched, and had lowered gazes. Were they spies, or criminals? They displayed those characteristics—if you assumed that the professions lived up to a movie reputation. But then someone who knew the city reassessed the five thousand hours. What the analyst had missed was that just out of the fixed shot was a Camembert factory.

The first lesson in seeing movie is for the filmmaker. Every time a member of the audience looks at any shot, or single frame, he or she will assume that everything in that frame was chosen, organized, and presented as a significant element of the movie, and that anything omitted does not exist. We say that such images partake of "composition." That kind of order is reassuring, for we realize, deep down, that the screen could show us anything it liked—shocking images thrown in our faces in brazen defiance of the thing called continuity. Luis Buñuel's *Un Chien Andalou* (1929) was like that, a short film that starts with a woman's eye slashed open with a razor and then pours a riotous stream of dream imagery into the wound. Why does she deserve that? Why do we? Because we were sitting patiently expecting order?

A key word here is "frame" and all it implies. In that Ray Bradbury story, "The Veldt," where whole walls are screens, the setup seems regular and controlled, but the lions don't share that understanding. The frame is the rectangular form that amounts to the window of cinema. In *Rear Window,* when Jeffries looks across his courtyard he sees a series of frames or screens, one or two for every apartment. It seems obvious that the frames separate the things inside them from those outside of them. But those externals take at least two forms: the contiguous space that we take for granted and which may have been in the frame seconds before in a panning or tracking shot; and the things that have no physical existence but which work as an idea stroking the facts of the story. The sound of wind is a good example of that. Thus, there is that difference between Orson Welles's emphatic abbreviation of Kane's death and the master shot I imagined that might show Kane's room in the context of Xanadu and the other people there who wait on his death. That is why our hearing "Rosebud" is so important, and why the opening of *Kane* takes place less in a particular room in a special palace, but instead in the mind of the dying man and the ambiance of forlorn wealth. The whispered word, echoing in his head, suggests the space at Xanadu is actually small, cramped, and like a cave.

The information counts for something—it always does. So the 2014 war film *Fury* took great pains over having a true-to-1945 Sherman tank, to battle those bad (but superior) German tanks. Maybe the best part of that film is in showing how five men lived inside the Sherman and had their war. But information is often warped by suggestion, poetry, and the demands of fiction. *Fury* is crazy in wanting to have pitched battles with German tanks and have us believe they are decisive enough to deserve Brad Pitt's time and our interest. But the art direction over the antique tank ignores the total air superiority the Allies had by April 1945. If the Germans had any tanks left, air strikes were called in to incinerate them. But that is history. So *Fury* is framed, and so are we.

For decades films were shot in what was called a golden frame, or an Academy frame, with a ratio of height to width that was 1.33:1. Just think for a moment of the meanings, or the antagonism to meaning, in a frame that is indefinite and not rectangular—a screen like a puddle, an impression, or a bloodstain—like the thing seen in dreams, or in life (for our vision, optical and imagined, is not framed). That golden frame is rarely used now and for a long time when films from that era were shown on television, the format was adjusted so that the height was rather less and the width rather more than was intended. Some television networks adhere to the old shape (Turner Classic Movies, for instance) and your television set may have a way of adjusting to the old shape. But for fifty years now, the format of films has been fudged on television.

The new medium always had a dilemma when it wanted to show formats that had been designed to defeat television. One of those formats was CinemaScope (begun in 1953), where the ratio was 2.66:1. That made for horrific renderings (known as "pan and scan") where sometimes the TV image of a Scope film was little more than the space between two people at opposite edges of the frame, perhaps with just their noses showing.

CinemaScope was the subject of many jokes, in part because it was a gimmick meant to distract us from television, but also because it became associated with empty spectacle, especially religious epics that were moribund in so many aspects of plot or content that the inert oblong (the letterbox, as it was called) was easily derided. A terrible slackness was felt, as one essential method of the filmmakers was squandered. As a result the viewer trusted nothing and looked less closely.

But Scope was as good as its material and its users. To take one example: Nicholas Ray's *Rebel Without a Cause* (1955), in Scope, is a largely interior story, set in southern California and concerning life in high school: it is the James Dean–Natalie Wood–Sal Mineo classic referred to earlier. Ray was one of the finest frame composers film has ever had; he had learned from Frank Lloyd Wright the beauty and energy of the horizontal frame, especially in domestic interiors where it might seem awkward or ill-suited. Ray used Scope to make rooms melodramatic and full of tension. *Rebel* is a film about emotional space in which the extra width is a way of emphasing the loneliness of characters, the claustrophobia of their family life, and the epic, romantic possibility of liberty or escape. I suspect Ray would have made as fine a film using the Golden frame (the way he shot *They Live by Night, On Dangeous Ground,* and *In a Lonely Place*), but he had Scope and he made it feel alive with unease.

That's what we expect of any screen format. But
begins in those shapes (the page format of a book
lar consequences). It's reasonable to say that *Rebel* i
matches the domestic space in affluent southern Cal
homes, just as it catches the loneliness of Dean's character lying
in the gutter awaiting arrest, the infinite grandeur in the Planetarium, and the peril of the clifftop "chickie run" that is a
crisis in the action. Equally, there is an astonishing moment
where the wide-angle camera represents Dean lying on a sofa
and then goes through a semicircle as he sits up. That sounds
excessive or like showing-off, but in the film itself it helps us
place Dean's character not just as a rebel but as the most sen-
tient being in the film. It is Dean's command of space that sub-
tly contradicts the film's title, for this is a story about a troubled
kid who *does* understand a lot about life, including the way his
parental generation (postwar America) has fucked up. He does
have a cause, and it involves life itself, liberty, confidence, and
purpose. On the page this may sound schematic, but on screen
it is something felt before it is understood.

You see, we feel the frame. Let me offer another example:
the films of the Japanese director Yasujiro Ozu, most nota-
bly his *Tokyo Story* (1953). Ozu made movies about family life,
settled hierarchies, and domestic interiors; they seem simple at
first, though the resignation of the characters, to fate or unhap-
piness, is often more demanding than the parables of happiness in American films. Nicholas Ray wanted to believe that
rebellion could remake the world—it has been an American
fallacy—while Ozu understands that melodramatic alteration
will be buried in time; that is his limitation.

Ozu usually shot in black and white with a golden frame.
He preferred static shots, where the camera did not move, while
human action toils within the still frame. That sounds formu-

laic and nearly ritualistic, but if you watch *Tokyo Story*—a film that could be fruitfully paired with *Rebel Without a Cause*—notice how much the stillness contributes to the feeling of enclosure. It is orderly, calm, and pleasing; yet there are hints of claustrophobia and confinement. The choice of framing is an immediate threshold to complexity, for it makes the rooms seem safe containers while never losing the prospect of prison. Ozu's way of seeing is humane and fair, to be sure, but it contains the seed of resignation and repression.

There has always been a struggle in the movies between having us feel safe, or ready for adventure. In *Locke,* say, the car interior is confining and oppressive, but its solitude gives Ivan a strange calm in which he can still feel he's captain of his ship. That struggle is rooted in experience, but it spells out the economics of the film business, too. Film has offered adventure, hope, fantasy, and escape for those of us encased in poverty, limitation, and quiet desperation. So the business of film gathered as many security routines as it could think of: you have to pay to get in; you should be there on time; you sit in a seat in a row of seats; the music is "movie music," which says here we go again; the picture has stars who are admirable in part because of their familiarity; and it has story structures like those we have known before. So it soon became a principle of factory filmmaking: do what we did before.

But audiences want it different, too. They want something they've never seen before. They want new faces, outrage, and the playfulness of danger, even though they don't want the locomotive or the wall of blood to come off the screen and into the auditorium. So many movies, and not just old ones, whisper to us about how they are going to work. It's like driving: on the roads we keep to one side of the road; we halt at stop signs; we observe certain speed limits; and we try not to crash into each other. Yet many movies about cars thrill to the breaking of all those rules—think of the car chases in *The French Connection* or *Bullitt*. Just as films say, Wouldn't you like to pretend you're shooting someone or making love to a phenomenal beauty, so they take our neurotic fears for our scratch-free cars and also say, Let's go wild! Driving is the only ease in Ivan Locke's life.

The headlong nature of film, the resemblance to a wild river or going out of control, is instructive. In the 1920s, in Paris, the leaders of the Surrealist movement were intrigued by movie. It was part of their credo to yearn for "automatic" elements in art—things not labored over or chosen, but taken at random or powered by a machine. Film seemed closer to that than any other medium. So they had a sport of going as a group to a cinema, not in time for the movie's start, but later on, so they arrived in the middle, fumbling and tripping in the dark. They sat down in front of the inexplicable action or plot and struggled to make sense of it—to turn sensation into information. They believed that made them attentive to the essence of cinema and appreciative of the power of mystery. But then, after ten minutes or less (for as early as the 1920s movies worked in habitual ways), when they agreed that they had worked out what was happening, they got up and left. But they went down the street to another movie house and entered that dark and its unfathomable story—until they knew where they were. Then they escaped again.

Does that sound absurd, expensive, and an irritation to others in a settled audience? It's not that far from the mood in which we go to a "new movie." Orson Welles said how, as a boy, he usually went into a film while it was playing and left when he realized that's where he had come in. That's harder now, because screenings are separated and punctuality is called for. But it's worth trying, for it opens the mind and sometimes makes us smarter—as well as "wrong." In January 1956, I went to see James Dean in *Rebel Without a Cause* (some films haunt our lives). I was fifteen and Dean had been dead for about three months. My desire to see him was such that I got there early enough to be waiting in the lobby with many other people for the next show to begin. Some rebellious impulse prevailed and I went in early.

The packed theater was quiet and tense. The CinemaScope screen was like a horizon where one might roam. We were in the Planetarium scene near the end (though I didn't know what it was, and I knew next to nothing about the story in advance). Plato (Sal Mineo) has taken refuge there. He has a gun. Jim (James Dean) goes into the building to talk him out. The police are outside with their guns and searchlights. What I saw was the young vulnerable face of Mineo and the seemingly older and more experienced look of Dean.

Now think of what I was seeing in terms of information: In 1955, when the film was made, Sal Mineo was sixteen, and Dean was twenty-four. Nothing had been done to hide that age difference in two alleged high-school seniors. Dean seemed older, more knowing, more in control, and whereas Mineo looked like a wild kid, Dean was groomed, nearly suave and elegant. If you look at that film closely, his carefully combed hair is seldom out of place. More than that—and here we get into delicate, difficult territory—Dean had a look of darkness in his face, a more fatalistic experience than Mineo had yet had. He was like an older brother to the kid.

Jim asks Plato for the gun—to look at it. Plato is unsure, but he wants Jim to like him, so he passes the gun over. Unseen by Plato, Jim slips the bullets out of the gun and then gives it back to Plato. In the whole arc of the film, this is a protective gesture, meant to save the boy. But what I had seen in isolation was a ruse, a way in which an older person had deceived a kid. It was one mind manipulating another, and that small piece of action seemed to fit the brooding disquiet in Dean's face and his bearing. It would always affect my vision of him as not just an achingly sincere, misunderstood young man, but a watchful, withdrawn master of events, full of purpose and calculation. He wasn't just a lost character; he was a budding director. There is a scene in the earlier *East of Eden* where his character, Cal, deliberately takes an older but more innocent brother to see the whorehouse mother (Jo Van Fleet) they have never been told about. It is a scene full of power, vengefulness, and malice, and one of the best things Dean ever did.

In *Rebel*, Plato panics. He rushes outside, gun in hand, and is shot down by the police. There is then the agonized image of Jim shouting out, "I've got the bullets." It's a tragedy once you see the whole film (and maybe it is Jim's tragedy as much as Plato's), but I never lost the feeling that Jim had arranged it so. That was my mistake, I'm sure, or not what the director Nicholas Ray intended. But a depth of movie expression has little to do with being right or wrong. There are layers of information or feeling that are not in the script and which may never have been spelled out. In other words, Ray believed in elements—of life, light, passing time, place, chance, gesture, whatever—that were not always under his control.

Control and its opposite—that tension goes all through the history of movies. The control covers the technology (more or less incomprehensible to most viewers) and the fixed frame. But the opposite can be improvisation, the infinity of performance, or simply the untrammeled beauty of movement within the frame (think of the implied lewdness in the way Groucho walks—I'm not complaining). It can be the unmediated passage of time and distance. Of course, nearly always it is a fusion of the two where we are almost obliged to assess the balance if we are watching closely. There are directors who seem to have a famously open liberated style, waiting on the vagaries of behavior, light, and time—Rossellini, Altman, Renoir, Antonioni, and many documentarians. And there are disciplinarian directors who want to control or direct our experience as much as possible: Fritz Lang, Sergei Eisenstein, Alfred Hitchcock, Stanley Kubrick. Up to a point, this is a useful distinction, but only if you're ready to recognize the contradiction it contains.

Hitchcock seems like the epitome of control: he liked to envisage every shot of his films in advance; he wanted to have his storyboards turned into film; he was persistently nagging us on how to look; it may have been his teasing superiority, but he sometimes declared that he found the actual shooting of a film rather boring; he preferred to cast known quantities who hardly required direction. As much as any director, he seems to have supervised everything; even so, an element of suggestion cannot help but creep in. It is so strong that one has to believe he at least stayed awake during the shooting. He loved to look. And I suspect nothing frightened him as much as loss of control.

Consider the first thirty minutes or so of *Psycho*.

Marion Crane is a secretary in a realtor's office in Phoenix, Arizona. Let us say she is thirty-two, the age Janet Leigh was when she made the picture. She has a man friend, Sam Loomis, who lives in another town far to the north, Fairvale, California, where he works in the hardware business struggling to pay alimony to an ex-wife. Sam and Marion lack the money to be together, but they have managed a lunchtime assignation in a shabby hotel room in a sunless Phoenix (something you have to wait for—Hitch seldom gives nature a break).

Marion is in control of herself, but troubled. When she returns to the office, on the Friday afternoon, her boss has just settled a large deal and he asks Marion to deposit the cash in the bank quickly. She goes back to her apartment; she changes clothes; and then she drives out of town with the money. She is active, but control has gone. She is headed for Fairvale, and she sleeps by the roadside. When a cop wakes her she becomes increasingly nervous about what she has done. It was an irrational action, though she seems to be a sensible person. She trades her car in an abrupt, foolish way. As the hysteria of her action mounts, she is losing more control. She begins to imagine the voices of her boss and others working out what happened. It starts to rain on the highway, adding to her stress and fatigue. And then she sees a neon sign in the dark, a motel sign saying "Vacancy." She stops to stay the night. She is "home"; she is lost.

More or less, that's what police evidence might be at the inquest: the cut-and dried facts of the case, the information. It's not that it's incorrect. But it's less than the movie. Let's list some of the other "movie" elements that inform us on how to think and feel.

1. The film is in black-and-white, and by 1960 that was a decision that went against normal practice. Further, the black-and-white is more harsh than rich. It's a little abrasive on the eye, not comforting or beguiling. This would be a different film in color: Marion would have real skin; colors in her clothing—would you want her in white, black, red, or yellow?

Arizona and California would have to acquire the hues of desert, forest, mountains, and sunlight. Nature would creep into the film and life would be a little gentler.

2. It's Janet Leigh. What does that mean? Well, Leigh was beloved in 1960. She was attractive, amiable, Californian, with a sense of humor, and a very good body. That information is touched by opinion, of course, but I think you would agree with my account of the actress if I ask, What would *Psycho* have been like with . . . Kim Novak, Grace Kelly, Audrey Hepburn, or Anne Bancroft, all of whom might have been in contention for the part? Novak—intriguing, more helpless than Leigh, seemingly not as smart; more sexual; maybe a little more vulnerable. Kelly: too smart, too witty, hardly fit for Phoenix or a secretary's job, hardly prepared to settle for the occasional lunchtime sex session, or for John Gavin, who plays Sam Loomis. Hepburn: maybe, interesting, a victim to be sure, but she's not quite sexual or common enough, and is she impulsive enough to steal the money; above everything, could anyone bear to see Audrey hacked to pieces in the shower? *Psycho* deals in cruelty, but there are limits. Bancroft: very interesting, because she's odder, brunette, not really starry, and she could bring out the irrational neurotic qualities in Marion. We might have no doubt about Bancroft: Marion Crane would be the psycho.

3. Or Anne Heche? She played Marion in the 1998 remake, directed by Gus Van Sant. That *Psycho* is a travesty, but Heche is a good actress (arguably subtler than Janet Leigh, if colder). So Marion becomes a very different figure in a film that never performs. To see the remake is to understand more fully what Leigh's genial star persona contributed—not least in the abruptness of her removal. In the original film, an appeal-

ing woman is murdered. The remake merely disposes of Anne Heche, who is a blonde in a color film and more believable as a half-desperate secretary.

4. So it's Leigh, who brings her own qualities: she is blonde, and being blonde in black-and-white has its own force. What is that quality exactly? It's hard to say, but impossible to miss. She has experience, much more than innocence. By 1960, Leigh had two children. She was married to Tony Curtis, and they had been a favorite item in the media in pictured embraces where it was impossible to escape the conclusion that Janet and Tony were having fun. Moreover, Tony was her third husband. Leigh's first marriage had occurred, in Reno, Nevada, when she was fifteen, and it had been annulled a few months later. Leigh was experienced: when the client in the office propositions Marion, Leigh's eyes know exactly what he intends. This is delicate territory, even if Janet Leigh has been dead for a while. I met her a few times and I'd say she was appealing, insecure, and anxious to be liked. IMDb says she had "a voluptuous figure." That's how it struck me and that is certainly how she had been photographed over the years.

5. It's how she is regarded in *Psycho*. The police evidence omitted a few things—like the way she is first seen in the film, stretched out on a bed (with the camera at bed level) in a white slip and a white bra (and a bare midriff). Now this was 1960, when that coded information was easy to read: sex had been had, and enjoyed (which does put it at the level of a meal or a sauna—movies are not often much good on the inwardness of sexual satisfaction). Also, this was what the film showed us after a very striking opening in which the camera had closed in on the drab building in Phoenix and slithered in through six inches of open window to discover Marion on her back on the

bed with Sam above her naked to the waist. And because it was 1960, we did not see their sexual activity—which made it that much more repressed and desirable.

She could be shown in other ways: she might be dressing or doing her hair—the purposeful secretary on her way back to work; she could be splayed out, from a high-angle view, meat on a morgue slab or a body for hire; she could be face down (that might permit no bra) as if exhausted or depressed; she could be asleep; she could be gazing out of the window at the wretched city of Phoenix. But no, she is on her back, composed, still, sexual but not flustered or disheveled. There's something insolent, not in her, but in Hitchcock whispering to us, Well, you know what's happened, but you're not allowed to see it. You'll have to imagine it. Put like that, you can feel how the film offers her as a prize we will never attain.

6. As the film advances, it becomes apparent that the framing of the photography is intense and claustrophobic. Those may be imprecise terms, but if you go through *Psycho* shot by shot you can point to the exact remorselessness with which Hitchcock visualizes the action and oppresses Marion. He treats her as a kind of target, or a victim in the making. A reinforcement of this are those scenes where she is driving, compelled to look straight into the camera, while being grilled by voices on the sound track. The headlights of other cars serve as a version of the third degree. This only schools us for talk in the motel meeting with Norman Bates about people living in their traps.

7. Note, too, that the several other characters we meet (all small parts) make a gallery of rather unpleasant people: the coworker in the real estate office (played by Hitchcock's daughter, Patricia) is crass, vain, and intrusive; the boss is anxious and chilly; the client in the office is a drunken lecher who wants to

get Marion in bed; the policeman on the road is a peaked cap and dark glasses looking straight into the camera; the used car salesman is brisk, clichéd, suspicious, and opportunistic. Five cameos and a world of abrasiveness, so that Marion has been abraded throughout, which only makes it clear how Norman Bates—the motel man—is kind, thoughtful, sensitive; he's Anthony Perkins.

8. In the most incriminating moment so far, when Marion decides to take the money, and when the envelope holding it is resting on top of her bed, she is undressing again. She abandons her office outfit for traveling clothes that include a black slip and a matching bra. The body is there again. That's twice, and missing from the police evidence. Well, so what, you say, she's got to wear something—except that you are wearing something now and we haven't mentioned it, let alone seen you in it (because you're not in a movie). Also, there will be a third disrobing for Marion, the most complete, as she takes off all her clothes before entering that merciful shower at the end of her long day on the road (after she slept in her car the night before).

Now, these numbered levels add plenty to the basic information offered by the police. Not that I have mentioned every level: for instance, the music, by Bernard Herrmann, has not been featured yet. We'll come to music, which may be the hardest thing to write about. And we'll come to cutting, which clearly is relevant to a film devoted to sharp blades.

It's temping to say that a camera is always a source of detachment and objectivity: when the camera moves in on that building in Phoenix with date and time, there is a hint of surveillance footage, and you can imagine the dry voice of a cop (Joe Friday: "Just the facts") delivering the information. But as that camera sneaks in through the open window, the film picks up a feeling for the furtive and for voyeurism. In other words, the detachment—the film, if you like—is saying, Come and see what I can show you. Be enlisted, and that old feeling of privilege is touched on again—should we be looking? Well, don't you want to see?

Especially in 1960, *Psycho* built up an erotic urgency that had to do with Janet Leigh, those bras and her breasts. You can call this pressure old-fashioned and sexist. Isn't it asking why a thirty-two-year-old who looks like Janet can't get laid as often as she likes? Isn't it also hinting that maybe we could do that laying?

Now, Marion is our central character. She is embodied by an actress we like. We sympathize with her tough day and her less than ideal life. We can understand why she thought of absconding with the money, and we feel (even if we do not note it) that the irrational impulse is linked to her sexual frustration. She is not a bad girl, just stressed. We follow her through the lengthy, touching, and beautifully handled conversation with Norman and we feel her regaining calm and balance. We like her all the more for deciding to go back to Phoenix the next day and return the money. We wonder how that will work out. We may even have a suspicion that she and Norman could become a couple. I know, Norman is odd, and he seems a victim of loneliness and that domineering mother we have heard in the distance up in the house that looms over the motel. It's not that Norman is Mr. Right, but he's righter than the other people in the movie and he's more tender to Marion's inwardness than Sam Loomis is. Who knows which way it will go? But in 1960, Janet Leigh was the star of the film, so presumably it would go with her.

Let's not be coy. You know what happens. Control has gone; a shy control freak has moved in. We are then asked to witness what is still one of the most shocking disruptions in an American film. I should add that *Psycho* is now fifty-five years old. That's a long time in movie history and there's no shame in something dating badly. It was made in 1960, the same year as *Inherit the Wind*, *Spartacus*, *The Alamo*, *Can-Can*, and *Sons and Lovers*. You can watch those films again, but it has to be on sufferance. So many conventions that worked then have been wiped away. Those films are no longer as suspenseful, as frightening, as exciting, as funny, or as inspiring in the moments when they were meant to be. But the shock of the shower scene has not abated.

You can say that the shower scene is effective because of Hitchcock's fastidious control—all those very short shots cut together so that (as he boasted) you never see a knife piercing flesh. That's true, and in the very rich sound track of that scene, the music screams, the water rushes, and you can hear and feel a blade biting flesh. So you can praise the film technically, as screen storytelling.

But that won't convey what has happened in the thirty minutes: we like Marion Crane and are rooting for her, but we also want to see her get some sexual delivery and satisfaction. We have become accomplices in the film (this is Hitchcock's most cunning and intimate skill) so that we can feel for the victim and the killer at the same time. This is far more than a conventional play upon the Jekyll-and-Hyde duality in most of us. It has to do with the structure of film as an experience, the marriage of intense actuality and magical detachment, so that we have a truly divided self. It is the way in which information can hardly exist without being emotional. And it is why the greatest test in watching movies is to respond to the plot or the characters, while observing film process, too.

Anyone who has written about film, and taught it, recognizes those moments where someone comes up to you and says, "You know, I appreciate a lot of what you're saying and I find it very interesting, but it's taking me out of the story, out of the movie. I find I'm watching the camera more than what it shows me."

I sympathize with that predicament. But my reply is that a little perseverance will be rewarding. When you read a novel, you are not actually lost in the story—you know your place in the text. If you drop the book you can find where you were. The "story" exists only as a conceit between the words on the page and your imagination. This happens quite naturally, and our history at the movies—our experience of the business—has been to believe we should relax, take it easy, sit back, and enjoy ourselves. But people cannot enjoy themselves without thinking about it. You may say to yourself that sex is purely physical, and it may be one of the most direct sources of pleasure we know, but we don't reach that conclusion without thinking about it. The most erogenous zones are all in the brain.

7

WHAT IS A SHOT?

Once upon a time, giving a camera to a kid marked a coming of age, so young people thought of taking a photograph as a personal advance. Today we all have phones that snap anything and everything. So selfies are as casual and disposable as chatter. It *is* the new talk. But suppose you want to take a picture of your girlfriend. Why? Well, there is still a way in which fond photos hope to establish a relationship as a way of saying, Look you're beautiful—and I have *seen* it.

Possessing a photograph is not owning a person, but it is a step in that direction, and if you start to study the way people display portraits in their home or in their life you may learn more about the family dynamic than is comfortable. Photographs are helpless testaments, but they can be possessions. The art critic John Berger was among the first to notice that a photograph evoked both presence and absence: it reminds you of a person, but it underlines the way the person is not there now. Perhaps sometimes it's easier to love a photograph than a person.

So the girlfriend says, "Wait a minute," because she wants to look her "best" or most like herself. She thinks to brush her hair; she realizes not long after that that she might as well have a shower. She may have a "natural" attitude toward her appearance, but equally she might consider going to a hairdresser, the beauty parlor, or a shrink. "You're sending this picture to your parents?" she asks, when she has gentle, vague, but undeniable designs upon them. She wants to impress them. So she wonders next if she may need to buy a few new clothes. To be sure, she feels happy and at ease in her old black jeans and the cherry red shirt—and it's not that she doesn't look pretty or cute like that—but this photograph is meant to last a long time and it is to be the first thing his parents will see. Granted she may not have made up her mind yet about you. Still, having your picture taken is no minor matter; it is a gesture toward gravity. She may not be afraid of having her soul stolen by the blink, but perhaps she is bound to assess the likelihood and temperament of her soul. "Don't make the cherry shirt look too . . . well, you know, 'sexy,'" she asks, when she was the one who chose that shirt in the first place. (How would you like a documentary film of Anna Karenina buying her clothes, trying them on, deciding what suits her? Doesn't any actress playing Anna go through the same process?)

Who knows? This "cherry" shirt (some say "blood red" or "saucy pink") may be the brief, preserved moment that you and the children to come will gaze at for decades—*prepare yourself*—after she had that awful car crash. When there is an obituary, this may be the picture you give to the paper or which you print on invitations to the funeral.

"Do you want me to smile?" she asks. "Do you want me to look at the camera?" Immense aesthetic decisions descend upon you straightaway. You have become a director, just as she has taken on the role of herself, the one that never ends its run. This doesn't mean that either of you is a fake or dishonest: but you cannot carry out this simple matter without complex self-examination. In the year of *Anatomy of a Murder* and *Hiroshima Mon Amour*, the sociologist Erving Goffman wrote a book called *The Presentation of Self in Everyday Life* (1959)—if movies had subtitles, this might fit 85 percent of them, not to mention the way *Anatomy* and *Hiroshima* ask questions abut appearance and its reliability. Goffman's book identified a doubleness in our selves, which is not duplicity, but is so far-reaching it may threaten the eight-hour sleep of assurance or integrity.

We need not go into all the areas of choice in this simple snapshot—whether she looks off into the distance like a dreamer or grins at the camera with clenched candor. Whether she has her hair up or lets it drop down on her shoulders—so that you are inspired to wait for a breeze or have her shake her head, making the hair seem more alive. Whether you ask her to bare her shoulders and she refuses—"This is for your parents!" Still, the request lingers in her face; she is thinking about it, and sometimes a camera can grasp thought. So then when the shot is taken, she discards that rose red shirt and knows you're watching so that after just a few more shots you could be making love. Because if people want to look "nice" or their best in pictures, then they are likely to become lovable. One of the standard functions of the smartphone nowadays is to circulate candid inspection shots of boys and girls. Fifty years ago, maybe, lovers' snapshots had more tenderness or aspiration.

You may not think of yourself as a photographer (or director), but the camera does not permit that casualness. After all, you want the frame to be level. You want it to include your girl, and you can hardly help but make automatic adjustments in terms of what part of the frame she fills, and what else is in the picture. You are making a "shot." Do you want space in the photograph, and if so, where? And what does that space say about her if it is dark or light? Why not have her stand in front of the bougainvillea? Or the brick wall? Or the sea? No need to write captions for those settings, but each picture has a different potential for meaning. You can vary the lens. You can come in close so everything else becomes a blur, the sea and the bougainvillea just color washes. You can shoot from enough distance to show the line of her body ("Put your hand on your hip," you suggest) while giving a good idea of her face. You have to make sure of focus. You may even find yourself noticing the light, with the discovery that if she turns her head to the left and looks away with her head raised—such a good chin—the light and shadow frame her in a pleasing way. The sun and the clouds are helpers in all this, but if you had "lights" then you could make a whole world for her. Even if with an ironic touch, she might become a version of Marlene Dietrich in *Blonde Venus* or *The Scarlet Empress,* two of the films Dietrich made for Josef von Sternberg and which are among the most highly wrought movies ever shot.

You are making shots, and you are beginning to explore the range of choices that await professional filmmakers or artists. You can vow to ignore those choices, but the camera possesses all the material that will suggest decisions—it knows no other way. Cameras have been locked in fixed positions—Andy War-hol did that in his factory films in the 1960s, because he was only interested in a bare, unaccented record of the life in front of the camera. He was content to be boring, because he appreci-ated the unassertive charm of duration, or the passing of time. Surveillance cameras are unattended, but their vantage has been selected to match their impassive but untrusting purpose. And part of the imaginative character of surveillance is that empty authority or the foreboding neutrality which seems so indifferent to what people do even if it was set up to record it.

The formerly innocent still photographer may be stricken by these considerations. He may recoil from the discovery that the simple urge to "show" something or someone rapidly leads into an analysis of seeing and being seen. So what can seem like an unexceptional and unprofound wish to pass on an image is on the brink of a relentless examination of what it is you are seeing, and what you want to see. To that extent, the mer-est "shot" from daily life is not far removed from the scheme of shots in a film of maybe two hours and several interwoven narratives—perhaps even a work of greatness. Whether you like it or not, to choose a shot and "take" it is to leave a record of your own sensibility, just as a few lines of casual talk can lead to a searching analysis of your persona simply on the basis of vocabulary, grammar, and verbal construction. We are not good at being spontaneous or free from analysis. That may be why we love the idea of that freedom so much.

Let's look at a few moments from various films just to show the sort of decision-making that can go into a shot, and what that reveals about the temperament of a film. In Otto Prem-inger's *Laura* (1944), a young woman has been shot and killed. Her face was blown away. Mark McPherson (Dana Andrews) is the police detective on the case. He is a rough guy, intimidated by the classiness of Laura and her apartment. But he decides to spend the night there. Why? To learn more about the victim's life? Or to sink deeper into the lovely ghost of Laura? So he commands her apartment. He wanders around, and the moving camera is gentle and encouraging to his snooping. It lets him live there, and relax. He is drinking, dreaming. That works on us as well as on Mark. He looks at her underwear and her letters done up in ribbons; he sees his own rogue appearance in her expensive mirror; he stands beneath the large over-sweet portrait of Laura like a sinner come back to church. He falls in love with her, and in that heady, invasive process he drops off to sleep. Then there is a noise that wakes him—a door opening. A young woman comes into the apartment—it's Laura! (Gene Tierney). Has Mark's desire brought her back to life or has he crossed over into the spirit world? At this early point in the film, the very elegant shots that Preminger adopts leave rich doubt as to whether this is a murder mystery, the discovery of love, or a film about incipient mental illness. It feels like a matter-of-fact cop's inquiry, but it's trying to seize rapture.

At the start of *Gone Girl* (2014), there's a shot of a woman's blonde hair, as a man's voice talks abut her and her mysteriousness. The framing feels affectionate, but the man talks about cracking the head open to see the twists of brain. If that's worrying, then she turns and looks at him (and at us) with the special gaze of Rosamund Pike, the actress playing the wife. What can you say about an actor's face that is legitimate? Well, in this case, there is some assistance. The part of the wife was originally meant for Reese Witherspoon, someone we like, someone whose face may be just a little more known or accessible than that of Ms. Pike. The casting is important: Rosamund Pike is beautiful (whatever that means), candid but distant, cold, armored, and she comes without history. Her newness helps make that opening the best thing in an often hateful movie.

Now consider *Caught,* made by Max Ophüls in 1949. Leonora (Barbara Bel Geddes) is a rather empty-headed model who married Smith Ohlrig (Robert Ryan), a cruel, controlling tycoon. She leaves him and takes a humble job as a receptionist with Dr. Quinada (James Mason), who works for the poor. She likes the job and Quinada's dedication to underprivileged patients. She begins to find herself. One night after work, Quinada takes Leonora out. They are shy about dancing together, but then in one shot a tracking camera follows them across a crowded, smoky dance floor, the track seemingly driven by the music and their ease. We do not hear them talk. But by the time they come into the foreground of the shot, we know they have fallen in love. It is a scene of unforced simplicity or grace that uncovers new feeling in the story. Ohlrig always told her what to feel, but Quinada and the camera have let her discover it for herself.

We could have heard the two of them talk. The camera could be close and attentive, watching every flicker of emotion, with the other dancers passing by in the background. We could even have close-ups to register the deepening feeling in him and her. But Ophüls prefers the removed tracking shot, the ensemble of the dance, and a brief passage of time. He trusts to their silence and our anticipation. It takes just a few feet and twenty seconds or so for love to emerge.

This is one of the happiest moments in the work of a man usually certain that happiness was elusive and unstable—a breathless ecstatic tracking shot, carrying along the wife in

The Earrings of Madame de, say, could as easily lead to ruin as success. The more of Ophüls you see, the more persistent these tracking shots are. Some observers regarded them as ostentatious decoration, and even a way of masking slight, overfamiliar plots. But I think they were second nature for a man who thought and felt in terms of movement and who understood it as a map of passing time. The movements in Ophüls's films are like the beat of a heart or a clock. They are life being lived and running out. So finally, with Ophüls, the condition of movement is close to a passion. Movie is a plastic art. The very name equates motion and emotion. It is always a kind of dance.

The more searching and deeply felt the cinematic expression, the more open a movie is to resonance, layering, and contrary interpretations. The work of Renoir is an example of that, and its motto comes from *The Rules of the Game* in which it is said that everyone has his or her own reasons for what they do. The conflict in that, the untidiness or the chaos, emerges in the resolve to see people in groups instead of simplifying close-ups. Historically, and to this day, American film likes the close-up. So do we: it is the mainline into fantasy. But it has larger ramifications that have significance for democracy and liberty. As you watch, you cannot eliminate the undertone of philosophy even in a film that would shrink from that word. Or a photograph. There is a passport picture of Dr. Josef Mengele in which he looks kind, cheery, and thoughtful. In the age of photography we are all actors.

In John Ford's *The Searchers,* a female child, Debbie, has been kidnapped by the Comanches, in 1868. Her uncle, Ethan (John Wayne), goes in search of her. He is a harsh man, solitary, scathing, unfriendly, defeated in the recent Civil War, emotionally disappointed in life. He is accompanied in this search by Martin (Jeffrey Hunter), a half-breed attached to Debbie's family, and it is Martin who sees in Ethan's hostility the threat that he means to find Debbie and kill her because she has been defiled by marriage to a Comanche chief, Scar. All of this is seen against the terrain of Monument Valley (in southern Utah), a sacred place for the Navajo, and for John Ford and automobile advertisements.

The search lasts five years, so that Debbie is Natalie Wood by the time she is found, and evidently fit to be a wife—though she seems to have no children. There is suspense over how Ethan will act, but in the event he embraces his niece and takes her home. Nothing is as ambivalent as that homecoming. We are inside the homestead looking out at the brightness of the desert of Monument Valley. Everyone else enters the house, as Ethan steps back to usher them in. Then the moment remains for him to enter. All of a sudden, a film of many moods becomes not just coherent, but necessary. This is why it was made. There is a single shot—the door, the figure, and the light beyond. The camera exposure is set for the desert, so the threshold is dark and Ethan is a silhouette, although we can see enough detail in his face and stance to know that a filler light has been put up for him. (This is technical, but as you watch films more, so you become like a member of the crew.)

Ethan does not enter the house. Perhaps the emotion inside is too much for him? Does he want to be alone, or does he sense that he needs to be away from others? Has searching become habit? Has it made him an outcast? Has he recognized in himself the racist violence that came close to killing Debbie? Is he lonely or possessed by horror? Whatever our answer, all in one shot he hesitates on the threshold, then turns away, steps down from the porch onto the desert floor, sways as only Wayne could, moves into the ochre and orange expanse—until the dark door closes, shutting him out and ending the film.

Think of the home-movie footage Abraham Zapruder shot in Dealey Plaza in Dallas on November 22, 1963. He was not skilled, his camera was not refined, he had no artistic ambition. But his single-shot (486 frames) is not just the best record of what happened in those few seconds, it has been the template for explaining the event. It is chance cinema, documentary, humble, rough and ready, but maybe the most significant and reinterpreted film of the twentieth century.

These are just a few shots out of millions in the history of film; and for all except the Zapruder footage, let's say there were twenty or thirty alternatives, some of which may have been filmed and then discarded. There is no need for us to count the shots as we watch the film. But we cannot avoid the rapid process (twenty-four times a second, more or less) in which the supposed reality of a story is selected and taken for us, piece by piece. All I have tried to do in these few examples is to say that selection is not casual (not even when it has the air of absolute, insolent arbitrariness, as in some films by Jean-Luc Godard). It is as deliberate as the rectangle of our screen or frame remains firm. More than we may be able to articulate quickly, the patterns of this shot-making have entered our consciousness: so we know and feel the rhythm of crosscut close-ups in significant dialogue scenes; we are not surprised to hear the central logic of master shot and detailed close-ups that is used in filming countless scenes; we anticipate that shooting a character from the rear is likely to lead to some demon coming up behind them, goosing them or devouring them. We may not know the term "offscreen space" (a critics' favorite) but we feel its potential as easily as we expect the unexpected in life.

Just as we now know a certain number of plotlines by heart and habit, so the syntax of shot-making has gone into our nervous system. This is not necessarily good. The sheer tonnage of images and stories may have helped account for the tedium and predictability of much of the medium, and put a hysterical stress on novelty for its own sake. So picture-making acquires a mad imperative: show us something we have never seen before, even if that thing is "impossible" in life.

That matter of possibility, or its opposite, is highly important. For decades, audiences responded to movies as they had done to photographs for fifty years or so before the stills began to move. They trusted them. They agreed with the implicit contract—*that is* Lincoln, or Walt Whitman—and they abided by the progress apparent in such shots. It is part of our fascination with Lincoln, and our respect for what he did, that we have still photographs taken over the last few years of his life that could be stills in a movie about a leader's fatigue, his doubt and difficulty, his illness (perhaps), and the aging that accompanies such responsibility. It's easy to say that Daniel Day-Lewis was outstanding in Steven Spielberg's *Lincoln,* though that may be undercut by the certainty that he would be that good in advance. To this day, however, despite the skill and dedication with which Day-Lewis made himself a version of Lincoln, I believe the still pictures from the 1860s are more moving. Day-Lewis may be more impressive, or spontaneous, as Daniel Plainview in *There Will Be Blood*—because he is the original Plainview, unhindered by questions of resemblance. One hundred and fifty years after Lincoln, it's easy to believe the man was playing himself in life. But Plainview is fresh, insane, and dangerous. On screen, I think I prefer him (though it's better that Plainview was not president).

So the great impersonations of early cinema—Paul Muni as

Zola or Pasteur or Juárez (how could he look like all of them while maintaining integrity?)—have paled and dated compared with, say, the increasing effort in Gary Cooper to look like Gary Cooper. That man aged and seemed to suffer in the way of Lincoln in the still pictures. Go from *Morocco* to *Meet John Doe* and from *The Fountainhead* to *Man of the West* and you cannot miss the way, shot by shot, time has eroded beauty, confidence and perfection. In turning up to be photographed, to be shot, Cooper was doing something that transcended acting. He is in the company of Rembrandt or Lucien Freud looking at themselves in the mirror.

That sense of plain life revealed on film was a vital part of the pact with reality implicit in movies. In our time, that pact has been increasingly qualified by special effects, by digital photography, by electronic images generated in the computer. To say the least, we do not trust the shot in the way we did, as a record or an imprint of reality. That has changed moviegoing along with so many other aspects of our culture. But the promise of life is still there, and still honored in many films.

One of the gross restrictions on liveliness in our movies is the pressure under which something, always, has to be *happening*. A kind of claustrophobia can result; you can feel it in Hitchcock and in every commercial ever made. And the dominated eye can wither the soul. Whereas I love that air of indolence or indifference that can come from just looking at time passing, and asking yourself, is something happening?

If we go back to our starting point in this chapter, to a photograph of a girlfriend, we know the feeling that while some pictures are adequate records of the appearance of the person who was "shot," others "get" her—they reach into the inner life or soul; they make us want to *look*. That may be because you learned as an amateur to manage the light and the composition in novel ways, and because the girl loved you and felt that the act of photographing her was a measure of trust so that, for an instant, she looked away at the light and thought of nothing except that her life depended on the moment—more or less that is what Josef von Sternberg asked of Marlene Dietrich in their films together. That is what turns a snapshot into a picture, or an ordinary photograph into a shot. It is in taking exceptional, penetrating pictures that most camera-handlers discover the desire to be photographers and what it is to look with depth. In the same way, any attempt to write is going to feel the resonance of words and sentences. So the record of life becomes an attempt to understand it. A shot is always that attempt, so long as we are watching closely. A film teaches us to see, and the shot is its mechanism. You can say it's like a word, but that's too crude. Sometimes a shot is a sentence—or a book.

As if that were the whole thing.

8

WHAT IS A CUT,
AND DOES IT HURT?

A shot might run forever, or as long as life. Sometimes you feel that urge in its momentum. It's part of the fluidity in film and the modern sensibility of surveillance. That Zapruder film from Dealey Plaza concludes when the motorcade races away to the hospital, and Zapruder surrenders to the shock of what he had witnessed. But our curiosity about that terrible day wishes the shot could be endless. If it could have begun earlier, and known to pick out some special places (if Hitchcock or Scorsese had been in charge). If it had been thorough surveillance; if it had scrutinized every possible shooting spot—then the motorcade might have been stopped. You can anticipate the discipline that follows in a future security system that sees everything.

A tracking shot—working in space or time—is an exploring wonder. But how will it terminate? Jean-Luc Godard once said that every beautiful tracking shot—even those by Max Ophüls—contained the seeds of its own destruction. It had to stop eventually, and in practice that required an imperative of story. It's like the tracking shot with the car at the start of *Touch of Evil:* it almost requires a bomb. For a brief period, in the late 1940s, Hitchcock fell in love with endless shots and the prospect of unbroken film. So he shot *Rope* as if the entire thing were a single shot. The result was tedious and clumsy, but ostentatious, and in a few years Hitch regained confidence in his own natural talent for cutting.

It's the same with sentences. No matter how sweeping the current of words, the reader is impatient for a full stop, and the chance to try another. But in shooting and cutting, just as much as with talking and pausing, we can begin to feel the deepest rhythms of story, process, seduction, or attitude. When Ernest Hemingway's work had its first impact, critics spoke of naturalism, terseness, visualization, and simplicity; and some saw this as a writing affected by watching movies. But only if you agreed that movies had cuts, or edits, or joins; and only when you appreciated that that linkage had rhythm. (In this paragraph just ending—this one—you have to read sentences, and even ideas. But you must read punctuation, too.)

At the start of Jacques Demy's *Bay of Angels* (1963), the camera begins on the figure of Jeanne Moreau walking at dawn on the promenade at Nice. Then (on a car) it races away from her until her pale, nervy figure—she is in white with platinum blonde hair in a black-and-white movie—is lost in the distance. It is not that she removes herself; it's fate or traveling that lets her vanish in the crowd. All of this is accompanied by a cascading piano score by Michel Legrand, an accompaniment that feels as sustained as a river in spring. It doesn't matter what the shot is meant to mean (in terms of some tidy caption). The momentum doesn't bother with literary equivalence. It's so exciting that you feel it could go on forever in a movie called "One morning in Nice, I saw this woman . . ." But, then, sooner or later (and often as if we willed or wished it), the screen cuts to some other image and a story settles in about this woman, a chronic gambler, and the young man who will be altered by her way of life. Once the story is indicated, that piano music could be the roulette wheel, or its exhilaration in her head. And the steady diminution of her figure could be suggesting, one minute you're a winner, *the* winner, and then you start to be forgotten. But don't worry too much yet about what the shot means. Just go with the flow and wait for the cut that will begin to tell us whether that flow is a gentle stream or a racing sea, and whether we are the sturdy skipper in command, or swept away.

Now, in the days of moving film, shot at twenty-four frames per second (or whatever), the celluloid strip, if you had been able to examine it, was so many still pictures, one after the other. But separation was elided and replaced with continuity and duration because if you ran enough frames a second the eye and the brain attending saw life, or something so lifelike there was not much distinction. That was called persistence of vision. I put it that way because in finished prints of those movies, a cut is exactly like the gaps between frames. The gap may be an enormous jump, going from T. E. Lawrence's hand held over a flame in Cairo, to the immensity of the desert. But it is one frame after another on a strip of film. It is only in the editing of a film that someone took physically different shots, trimmed them, and then spliced them together, with film cement. Work prints composed like that would only go through the projector if the splices held. So the cut was also a splice, a coming together, a marriage.

This is not just playing with words. It's raising an issue that goes to the heart of the nature of movie—and it is something violently, but creatively, opposed to the philosophy of the endless shot. "Once upon a time" can suddenly become twice upon a time. Something else springs from that: most films, cautiously, will play it safe with time: begin at the beginning and advance to the end (*High Noon, All Is Lost, Twelve Angry Men*). But one film we've noted already, *Citizen Kane,* begins at the end and then comes back to the end from several different directions. Time is the playground of the movies—if you're alert enough to play there.

The word "cut" is tricky. It makes people think something has been omitted or excised. Once upon a time nudity was cut out of films; sometimes nowadays it is deliberately added in. But a director and an editor work toward a cut that is an assembly—the editing is done to create meanings, not omit them. The "director's cut" is now a precious contractual right, eagerly sought and often infringed upon, so sometimes the director's cut is only seen on the DVD release. Films like *Heaven's Gate* exist in different versions in which, far from being cut down, the idea of the film expands. There is "lost" footage from *The Magnificent Ambersons* that every film scholar has longed to find for over seventy years.

In film today, there is an intriguing clash between cuts that specify or focus an action, and those that let possibilities flower. When Terrence Malick made *Badlands* (1973) he cut the scenes of the runaway kids on the prairie to be precise and anecdotal, though he loved the openness of them dancing in the car headlights. But in *The Tree of Life* (2011), the cuts shift from family life in Texas in the 1950s to prehistory or the distant future with disarming ease. So sometimes Sean Penn in modern dress seems to be gazing at dinosaurs. Just a hundred years earlier people had stumbled on the basic link: he looks—he sees her; two shots that might have been made months and miles apart but which seem fluent on screen. In *At Close Range* (1986), there is a simple scene where teenage Sean Penn meets Mary Stuart Masterson. We know this kind of moment inside out. It is handled in crosscut close-ups; the two kids "act well" or they had something for each other. Who cares?—you can't watch without falling in love with editing.

At other times in the work of editing, when story problems arose, the looking shot might be cut with a mate that was never intended in the script. Yet still it works. You have to have spent time in a cutting room to appreciate this dynamic magic and the way it can confound, betray, or rescue shooting. But those cuts in *The Tree of Life* have led Malick from narrative to philosophy. The only question is, Can they carry an audience along with the ease and soaring desire from that bit of *At Close Range*?

It comes to this: the cut in a movie can be violent, transformative, and intimidating. Once we realize that a film can cut quicker than we can see—for we do not exactly see the join, just its impact—then the cut is a blade hanging over us, like a guillotine. That application is most evident in films that seek to frighten us. The appearance of the woman through the blurry shower curtain behind the oblivious Janet Leigh in *Psycho* is done within a shot—and it is one of the most frightening moments. But once the sequence gets under way, the line of the film becomes a series of savage cuts that mimic the thrusts of the knife—although the cuts also allow us *not* to see a blade cutting flesh, which would have meant trouble with the censor in 1960. But the violence of the editing and the jagged, wounded force of the surviving shots is all part of the way Hitchcock has constructed *Psycho* for shock effect. And once Hitch has cut to the knife in the shower, any other cut is possible in the future—it could be a severed head in your bed, a horse's head.

So, perchance to cut is a perpetual threat. No such dread operates in theater, where we sit in a similar position with a spectacle contingent on physical possibility. In fact, in the theater (the fencing in *Hamlet,* say) the action tends to feel ponderous and stilted just because it is hobbled by pretending. But from the outset in cinema, infinite imagined (or undreamed of) possibility has been in prospect. The more a film cuts, and the more adventurously, then the readier we are for its astonishment. Some sense of dread or magic is never far away, not even in naturalistic drama. Those cuts can hurt, but they can transport and transform and they can heal old wounds.

On a cut, the man in the neorealist classic *Bicycle Thieves* has his worst fear realized: his bicycle is stolen—so he will lose his job. Could things be worse? Could the alien that menaced Sigourney Weaver all those years be lurking around the street corner? No, that seems far too fanciful an association for the Rome of 1948. But don't forget that this impoverished man's job is pasting up posters of Rita Hayworth in *Gilda*—life-size, voluptuous, fantastic, a cutaway in the same frame, and a surreal partner for his threadbare life, nearly as unexpected and "crazy" as the 1979 alien created by H. R. Giger. So edits can exist in the same frame. In Alf Sjöberg's *Miss Julie* (1951; and a woefully neglected film), the past and the present coexist in the same shot, the child and the woman side by side.

Another way of handling that subtlety is in another lost art, the dissolve, where one image becomes another. At the depth of his despair in *The Wrong Man,* the falsely accused Henry Fonda character starts to pray. As he does so, the image picks up another one, a dissolve, of the real criminal walking down the street, coming toward the camera, until his face occupies the exact space that was Fonda's seconds before. I don't honestly believe in praying, but I believe in those shots and their slow cut. It's also a moment in Hitchcock's career where one cannot forget the fact of his Catholicism and the impact a sense of guilt and chance had on him.

The same kind of impending future waits in comedy, too. Thus, Chaplin, Keaton, and Harold Lloyd (or M. Hulot or Jim Carrey) are all likely to encounter (or be) sudden and absurd hazards. What this entails is a constant promise of surprise and peril more akin to magic acts or sporting events than the deliberate advance and accumulation of stage plays and operas. It is one of the secret sources of an inspiring sensationalism at the movies; the other is the suggestion that "everybody" goes into that revealing dark for a miracle or a gotcha. For decades, that Metro-Goldwyn-Mayer lion was a promise of unimaginable intrusions or wildness.

Yet, for every gotcha cut in the history of film, there are probably fifty smooth or invisible cuts. In the origins of the medium, the "matching" cut was far more a means of engineering transition or flow, and those things are a way toward subtlety. D. W. Griffith is hailed as one of a pioneering generation that identified the singularity of shots and then found ways of assembling them as building blocks in a sequence so that an audience reckoned steady time had passed. It's akin to the realization that in a narrative you can put down one sentence and then move to another set somewhere else or in a different time, in which the gulf is bridged because interest or attention carries over from one to the other. Just read this passage from near the close of Scott Fitzgerald's *Tender Is the Night* (1934). It's a lesson in reading, that could only be filmed if read onto the sound track:

> Nicole kept in touch with Dick after her new marriage; there were letters on business matters, and about the children. When she said, as she often did, "I loved Dick and I'll never forget him," Tommy answered, "Of course not—why should you?"
>
> Dick opened an office in Buffalo, but evidently without success. Nicole did not find what the trouble was, but she heard a few months later that he was in a little town named Batavia, N.Y., practicing general medicine, and later that he was in Lockport, doing the same thing. By accident she heard more about his life there than anywhere: that he bicycled a lot, was much admired by the ladies, and always had a big stack of papers on his desk that were known to be an important treatise on some medical subject, almost in process of completion. He was considered to have fine manners and once made a good speech at a public health meeting on the subject of drugs; but he became entangled with a girl who worked in a grocery store, and he was also involved in a lawsuit about some medical question; so he left Lockport.

Notice how easily that short passage provides facts, as well as the unreliable report of facts, and the subsequent uncertainty, and the melancholy it leaves. It's the kind of fluent transitioning that makes the cinematic adaptation of good prose so difficult. Even in abbreviated form, to show the entanglement and the lawsuit would be over-obvious; the cut from one to the other would seem clumsy and melodramatic. If actors said those lines—"I loved Dick . . ."—they would be pregnant and pressing; but on the page they are intriguingly quiet, or casual. An emphatic enactment would miss the poignant chemistry of Dick's decline and Nicole's glimpses of it. Just because film is so deliberately constructed—shot first and then cut and gathered—it has a problem with ease and suggestion. For in truth not everything is visible, and Fitzgerald's opportunity to move in and out in a sentence is so light-footed and adroit. By contrast, the impact of editing often underlines an attempt at meaning or insight in a crude way. So filmmakers are always striving for the suppleness in writing. But it's hard for an artful movie to seem relaxed.

You could see that a hundred years ago in Griffith. He moved in two directions at once with cutting. He felt the suppleness and flow with which he could convey an anecdotal incident: the shooting of Lincoln, the attempted rape of Flora Cameron (Mae Marsh), the great battle—all from *The Birth of a Nation;* surely that ease helped audiences in the test of sitting still for a three-and-a-half-hour story (so long as enough arousing things were happening). But in his next film, *Intolerance,* this naïve inventor yielded to the literary and philosophical ambitions he had felt in editing. He discovered lofty comparison and never realized it was dumb repetition and far inferior to the comparisons and allusions that Joyce, Henry James, and Kafka were making at about the same time. Kafka wrote *Metamorphosis* in the year Griffith made *Intolerance,* but the eery simplicity of its opening was so far ahead of what film could do: "One morning as Gregor Samsa was waking up from anxious dreams, he discovered that in bed he had been changed into a monstrous verminous bug." Then again, could Kafka have been so swift and sly in words without the casual transitions he had noticed on screen? The ways in which writers started learning from film are so many and so likely to disprove reports of the death of the novel.

Griffith decided to have four stories in *Intolerance* that demonstrated . . . human intolerance: incidents in ancient Babylon; the time of Christ; the massacre of the French Huguenots in 1572; and a modern story (set in 1914) in which a young man is wrongfully convicted of murder and will be executed if word cannot reach the prison in that recent creation of movies, "the nick of time," or what we might call suspense.

Even in 1916, the scheme threatened the vitality of any individual story. *Intolerance* was a failure commercially just as *Birth of a Nation* had founded a new business. The comparison of various intolerances was thought fatuous and long-winded, pretentious and silly, no matter that the Babylon sequence had a spectacular palace set built at great expense at 4500 Sunset Blvd.—but without any real idea of how to use it, so the camera (in a balloon) just drifts across the immense façade like a gaping tourist. Far too much of the historical episodes seemed dull excuses for costume, décor, and the preachiness of Griffith's attitudes. But the modern story is a gripping display of conventional suspense in which the articulated rendering of action (through edited shots) is matched by the hectic or desperate crosscutting of the final race against time. Isolate that modern story (it stars Robert Harron, Mae Marsh, and Miriam Cooper) and it might be the most impressive work of Griffith's career.

Suppose that the audience for *Intolerance* was disconcerted by the yoking together of far-flung periods, but riveted by the intensity of advancing action in modern storytelling. The lesson for commercial movies (which Griffith had done so much to inaugurate) was don't be aggressively ambitious and let editing act as an accelerating force in story. We still benefit from that decision, in pictures like *All Is Lost* and *Amour* as well as television series like *Homeland* and *Breaking Bad*. In all of those works, we find ourselves wondering what happens next, even if some of the answers are fanciful (or absurd). But that is only part of the potential in editing, and now the adventurous filmgoer needs to understand the dynamic better.

Let me repeat, the cut is also a joining or a suture. Try this experiment: Select two items of a modest size that seem to have nothing in common and put them on the same table. Then invite a newcomer to study the table and suggest a connection between the two things. That person will never fail, because the human mind has a helpless but essential capacity for seeing connections or likenesses. The cut in film may serve as an interruption, a stroke or caesura, if you like; but the watcher will knit up the rift so quickly it is amazing. The filmmaker may break his own flow with a shot chosen at random. In the Surrealist literature, the classic absurd pairing involved a sewing machine and an umbrella—and the agility of the receptive mind finds a clue: they are both used in repairing appearance; in both, you press a knob and they come to life; they are companions in the hall closet. . . . They are metaphors!

It may seem far-fetched to consider a whole movie based on this kind of dissociation, though *Un Chien Andalou* (1929), by Luis Buñuel and Salvador Dalí, was made in such a reckless spirit. It is a sixteen-minute dreamscape on the theme of sexual awakening that obeys no kind of restraint or censorship. Primitive, childlike but intuitive, it digs into the subconscious like people in a desert seeking water. There is a modern surrealist who functions on the edges of the mainstream, David Lynch, who slips unaccountable actions into the narrative of his films: remember Dean Stockwell's character, Ben, in brocade and heavy make-up, miming Roy Orbison's "In Dreams" in *Blue Velvet;* or Betty's steamy screen test in *Mulholland Dr.,* which manages to be comic, banal, and erotic all at the same time. It's not that *Mulholland Dr.* "works" in the way that can be reduced to a map of itself, a listing of subtexual meanings. Far more, it exposes us to the wildness of association, without the frenzied atmospheric of horror. The magic of *Mulholland Dr.* is in its calm. In the long run that is the only way to disarm the shock in cutting.

Facing most of Lynch's work, some viewers are likely to feel degrees of bewilderment or outrage. Some may stop watching. But for others, the digressions or departures only deepen the emotional power of his films. And if you need reassurance, just use the remote to surf through channels on your television and notice the arbitrary, incidental but sometimes haunting beauty you uncover. It's often more captivating and liberating than any particular channel, and it's a reminder that the Surrealists reveled in automatic or random associations.

If Picasso had looked at *Guernica* after he had finished and yielded to a passing whim by adding a prostrate odalisque to the frame, unaware of the air raid and its damage (she could be playing cards with that young man in Chardin), it would still be all Picasso. It might be a greater picture, or one in which the gravity and anger of April 1937 were pierced by unexpected inappropriateness. But what is trite about *Guernica* now (compared with *Las Meninas*) is that the whole damn thing is against air raids. Aren't we all?

In François Truffaut's *Shoot the Piano Player,* a gangster

swears on his mother's life that a story is true, and Truffaut nonchalantly interrupts his own narrative with a cameo shot of an elderly woman suffering an apparent heart attack. In the mood of the French New Wave of the sixties, there was a lot of blithe subversion. When Jean-Luc Godard assembled *Breathless,* he found the film was too long and so he went through it again introducing the jump cut. That saved time but it also undermined the articulate serenity of every shot and pronounced that film (even film that was the truth twenty-four times per second—a Godard axiom) was whatever the cutting made of it. So the film bumped and jerked along to a new time scheme rather as years later Douglas Gordon would replace the dread and suspense in *Psycho* by distending every frame and second until *24 Hour Psycho* became a contemplation of the film process. Some say that remaking is ridiculous, but Martin Scorsese, for one, has had the habit for years of doing multiple printing of certain frames in order to stress one instant over another. This is stretching time, if you like, but it is a kind of cutting.

Cutting does reveal artistic character eventually, but it offers so many prospects. In *The Magnificent Ambersons,* in the strawberry shortcake scene with Tim Holt and Agnes Moorehead, Orson Welles trusted to do it in one shot. He may have filmed covering close-ups, but in the event he settled for duration, the actors, and even a kind of boredom. Not that he rejected shock cuts in his career—the huge mouth saying "Rosebud" at the start of *Kane* that cuts to the glass ball breaking on the ground; the alarmed cockatoo in Xanadu; and even the moment in the cabin scene in Colorado when the purposeful mother walks across the room, throws up the window, and the film cuts to a sudden close-up of her face looking out at the cold and her son with a reordering of the spatial rhythms in the scene. For the cabin scene had been shot so far in a way that had no close-ups or their direct confrontation with emotion. It is a scene about actual interior space and the way the mother controls it. It is still debatable whether that sudden cut to the mother is to push her sensibility into the story (we hear faint music and a mournful wind and Agnes Moorehead cries out "Charles!," calling him and condemning him, as if the word had been torn from her) or to raise the unanswered question—what does her son think of her and of the way he was sold off? That implication is at the heart of the film's elusiveness, for the viewer was asked to understand the complex editing scheme of flashbacks and be able to balance them like the different narrative voices in Faulkner's *The Sound and the Fury.* (That entirely unfilmable book was written by a man who was about to become a Hollywood screenwriter.)

So many films liked to reassure audiences with the notion that the wild screen was manageable and organized. The prospect of abandon, orgy, madness, and slaughter touched on in *Un Chien Andalou,* in Russian and German film, was palpable and alarming. In Hollywood, even, it affected Stroheim and Sternberg. But the business was always anxious to keep that energy reined in, or unappreciated, if only so that business could stay regular and businesslike. Stroheim's *Greed* had been obstructed because it was excessive (it was cut from ten hours to two), but it was feared because of its direct assault on such a subject.

But in 1915, the editing ambition of *Birth of a Nation* had helped prove movies as a business and led to the building of theaters and the foundation of companies that would be household names. Yet if that picture is screened, for its anniversary, in 2015, in Memphis, in Atlanta, in Chicago, in Harlem, there will likely be demonstrations against its offensiveness. The phenomenon that established the show cannot be shown, except as a sign of history—and perhaps not even then.

For decades, mainstream filmmaking rejected cuts that might explore the full potential of cutting. That meant the denial of intellectual discomfort, and the elimination of a natural tendency for movies to seek the unknown. Apart from what it does to her in the shower, *Psycho* cuts Marion Crane's ostensible life into another not dreamed of until it happens (has she ever thought of being murdered?). But Hitchcock had always had his superstitious faith in the unexpected: it can range from Henry Fonda's being arrested in *The Wrong Man* to a plane dusting crops where none are growing in *North by Northwest*. In *Vertigo,* one can say that the James Stewart character sees a "cut" from one Kim Novak to another, but is slow in realizing how far the two women are married.

Any consideration of editing as a force that interrupts and fragments apparent order needs to take note of another condition in filmmaking. Very few movies are shot "in order," or according to the line of the narrative. For reasons of economic expediency, the shooting schedule goes all over the place. So the plot is disassembled for the actors; it is repeated, sometimes with many takes; and it is subject to reshoots, and the careful filming of extensive sequences (even entire locations) that never get into the final picture. So there is a natural and cheerful climate of the haphazard in film production, and a feeling of collage and alteration going on all the time. There is yet another nuance to this: the crazy schedule plays fast and loose with time, so that the things shot seem to be floating in just the way in *Kane,* say, you're never quite sure where or when you are.

At the very moment of *Vertigo* and *North by Northwest,* Alain Resnais made *Hiroshima Mon Amour,* expanding the reach in editing, and the right of film to use it. A French actress (Emmanuelle Riva) is in Hiroshima to make a film about peace. As she lies in bed with her Japanese lover (Eiji Okada) she tells him that she understands Hiroshima and what happened there. She has been to the museum. No, he says, she saw nothing. This is not a bitter dispute, but a calm assertion that Hiroshima cannot be understood in a museum or by looking at graves and signs. We assume a night of lovemaking between them. In the morning, the woman is up first. She has her coffee on the balcony and then she looks at the man in bed. His arm is rather awkwardly twisted against his body. There is a cut and we see another arm in a similar pose, but it is wearing a uniform. It is the body of the German soldier this French woman loved in a town called Nevers in a perilous act of collaboration for which she was punished when the war was over.

This one knot or synapse will be the motif of the film in which the woman speaks of loving Hiroshima and Nevers. Once that link is established, *Hiroshima Mon Amour* can move back and forth in time without awkwardness or effort. Once upon a time, the flashback was like a found object, a vital cache of letters or information, an answer in the mystery of story, a tidy package of life and action introduced for its explanatory value. But in *Hiroshima Mon Amour* the past is always there, untidy, sprawling, poetic, suggestive, and subject to errors of memory. (The present, the now, in film has to be correct; the past has no more chance of that than the future.)

The past may be the future. In Stanley Kubrick's *The Shining,* Jack Torrance has taken the job of caretaker at the Overlook Hotel to write the novel he has dreamed of for so long. He is alone there but for his wife and his young son. But the magnificent hotel is not comfortable when empty. It creaks with the possibility of story or ghostliness. Jack's writing is not going well, but he is desperate to be overtaken by fiction. He feels the pangs of his old weakness, alcohol, and prowls the corridors of the Overlook, drawn to the Gold Bar.

We have seen this place earlier in the film, alight and alive with customers, gold in its décor and in the sheen of the liquor bottles. The bar is there still, but empty and unstocked. Jack sits on a stool. His gloom mounts. He covers his face to shut out the world, perchance to dream. And when he removes his hands, on a cut, he sees Lloyd, the perfect barman (Joe Turkel), in front of shelves of glowing liquor. "What'll it be, Mr. Torrance?" asks Lloyd. The cut has restored the old trade of the bar and Jack's propensity for booze. But it is his future, too, the moment when ghostly story claims him for the Overlook and begins to detach him from his family. As a cut, it is both ecstatic and sinister, and the lesson of that possible marriage is not to be forgotten.

Cutting can hurt, or add an inadvertent panache to the violence it is dramatizing. For decades, Sergei Eisenstein was revered for the rigorously controlled, almost metronomic editing he used in the Odessa Steps sequence of *Battleship Potemkin*. Many of the townspeople of Odessa have gathered on the steps to cheer the mutinous sailors on their ship. Then the order is given for soldiers to disperse that crowd. In white tunics and black boots they advance with rifles and fixed bayonets. Their power is unstoppable and cruel. We see a woman's face slashed. We see screams—these are images that Francis Bacon used in some of his paintings. A baby in a carriage bounces down the steps unattended. There is no doubt left about the merciless violence of the soldiers and the suffering of the citizens. But

Eisenstein elects to present this action in tightly edited sections that fit together tongue and groove—a look of horror, the slash of a sabre, the line of jackboots. There is a drive and rhythm in the editing. No such effect had been seen before: this was the demonstration of a lot of Soviet theorizing over editing. It does have the stamp of a successful exercise. Almost involuntarily, the spirit of the sequence is shared between victims and tyrants. But the cutting enforces the attack of cold steel and amounts to a subliminal endorsement of it. Eisenstein never intended that, but as with so many brilliant theorists possessed by dynamic graphic talent, the sequence could get out of control. (Note: no massacre on the Odessa steps ever occurred, though it has passed into folklore by now.)

Similar tensions arise in Leni Riefenstahl's *Triumph of the Will* when she is glorying in the impacted mass of storm troopers and the eminent solitude of Adolf Hitler. Hitler is hardly photogenic, but the persistent celebration of his figure (with sunlight spilling in his saluting palm) is matched by the wall-like solidarity of his troops. And Riefenstahl is still condemned as a fascist artist. The use of what we call montage (radically organized material, constructed through the editing) in both films is ideological. It is akin to the dynamic cutting in King Vidor's *Our Daily Bread* (1934), where a group of farmers make a chain of water supply for a field.

Cutting can be a masking operation, an exercise in discretion. In the very candid love scene in Nicolas Roeg's *Don't Look Now,* the editing removed any glimpses of genitalia which the wholehearted actors—Donald Sutherland and Julie Christie—had to have revealed during their performance. That was their compact with Roeg, but it was a safeguard against censorship, too. Was it protectiveness that pushed Roeg to his finest measure? The lovemaking (unusually tender and free) is crosscut with events some twenty or so minutes after sex as the two of them repair their faces and dress to go out. It is an uncanny effect, and another playing with time, for abandonment rubs shoulders, and other parts, with composure. Nothing is said in *Don't Look Now*, where the looking *is* everything. No way of making the sequence could be offered in a novel, say. It is uniquely cinematic, critically reliant on editing, and inspired by time, film's most abiding and elusive subject.

Film wants us to see momentary things. It wants to show us something we have never seen before, and may not see again. Often, those glimpses turn on sex and violence. But those very topics have often led to distress and indelicacy. Pornography was not widespread in 1972 (the year of *Don't Look Now*), but now that it is an ocean we see how difficult it is to catch sexuality on film. It doesn't exactly photograph; it can't be seen or felt within the wrestling match of naked antics. So the authentic eroticism of *Don't Look Now*'s love scene is the more remarkable for the tension between modesty and explicitness, and its acuity in time. This may be the first lovemaking the couple have had since their child drowned, and it may be the last before the husband dies.

Nor can we really show a killing. There are still laws against such things, so the special effects of death have become hysterically ingenious. But suppose Hitchcock had said, Let us simply film the *Psycho* shower murder in one fixed shot—rather as Ozu might have done, or even as Hitchcock might have done it in *Rope*. So Norman would appear and stab Marion many times. Leaving aside the matter of the knife doing real damage, the simplicity of direct coverage would be intolerable. Norman's arm would weaken. Marion might gasp and urinate as her body gave way. Then the various degrees of censorship would have to intervene. And so the plain, unadorned brutality of a murder has hardly been shown in film. It is still the object of anticipation, dread, and desire; it is cloaked in that melodrama. So gradually, with time, we have come to respect murder more. Movie has given it a glamour that is unthinkable in life.

Of course, there are so many ways of being discreet and melodramatic, of cutting out the hideous instants, while letting pain and damage be implicit. But Hitchcock falls into the kind of trap that faced Eisenstein in *Potemkin*. He makes such an intricate, elaborate construct of the killing that his technical aplomb, his glee, cannot help showing. The murder is frightening, of course, but it is not free from Hitchcock's black humor or his pride at having managed it so well. He is a brilliant murderer. That is there in the surprise of the event itself and the technical mastery that boasts, I can show it without quite showing it. It is a set piece, a tribute to his own virtuosity and wit, and done with a flagrant artfulness that won't permit the censor to interfere in his razor-sharp cuts. It's the money scene.

What this opportunity to edit amounts to is one more intrusion on the alleged lifelike veracity of film. I asked you to appreciate that the simple shot—that lovely chance to see— was also an encouragement to analysis. That quest is redoubled by the potential of editing which is always ready to offset the level of actuality and to introduce a scheme of cross-reference. Put the two together—film and cutting—and we have a language so intense it is a marvel that we still teach our children to read, write, and spell, while omitting a curriculum that begins with an investigation of film. No wonder we feel adrift.

9

WHAT DO YOU HEAR?

Sound seems to complete the ghostly contract movies have with life. Now the process sounds like life as well as looking like it. But realize that sound is another kind of editing. Sound cuts into the picture; it adds music to the visual stream; it can insert a narrator's voice; it adds so many other nuances of sound effect to what we might call the silent film. You can experiment yourself. Take a famous stretch of silent film— try the opening of *Sunrise,* where the City Woman lures and seduces the rural husband to come out to the swamp. Run the scene with different types of music: Sinatra singing "I've Got You Under My Skin"; something from Debussy's *La Mer;* Donna Summer singing "Love to Love You, Baby"; the opening to the last movement of Shostakovich's Tenth Symphony; or a sitar raga played by Ravi Shankar.

That range is comic, yet they all work. Just about any music plays with any stretch of film, or any sound track: the *Sunrise* scene would play with a very heavy-handed "swamp" sound track—cicadas, hyenas laughing in the distance, and the sound of heat—I mean the pressure of sweltering atmosphere; or try it with just the mournful wind of the prairies and the creak of dry trees. The characters shift as we listen to them.

Different scores edit or organize a picture. They take it toward a different meaning: *La Mer* makes the adulterous affair lyrical; Donna Summer turns the film and its 1927 iconography into camp satire; Sinatra makes us chuckle over the sexual obsession; while the sitar begins to suggest that this small local infatuation—heady and damaging, perhaps—is just a pebble on a large beach.

As the "invention" of sound was labored over in the 1920s, the target achievement that obsessed its inventors was to make it synchronized: to have the sound of talk as lips moved; to hear the sound of a shot as we see the flash of a gun; and for the footsteps of Frankenstein's monster to match his movements on screen. That can be done. But in time filmmakers learned that asynchronicity had a point, too. So sound can begin two or three seconds before its proper sequence. A voice does not have to come from the mouthing face. And a particular sound effect can leap out of the overall naturalism of sound like a warning. In *A Dangerous Method,* Jung shocks and challenges Freud by anticipating that a cracking noise will occur, irrationally, in the room where they are sitting. The noise comes: Freud says it is accidental but explainable; Jung prefers to regard it as irrational but indicative. The auditory does not have to be a meek record of life any more than the pictures need to be accurate. Sound can have its close-ups and long shots.

Alfred Hitchcock was old enough to have made silent films. He had come into the business as a graphic designer. All his working life he spoke of "pure cinema," putting the stress upon visual storytelling and his own ability to angle shots and their compositions so that they seemed loaded with a psychological meaning that made talk superfluous. If he wasn't simply a purist, he was a meticulous craftsman willing to talk about filmmaking relying on visual manipulation, and being somewhere between a practical joke and veiled cruelty. Like many practical jokers he was seldom to be trusted. His *Blackmail* (1929) so straddled the coming of sound that it ended up being done in silent and sound versions. Hitch took a woman (played by Anny Ondra) who has stabbed and killed a sexual predator. He then had her mesmerized by a background conversation in which the recurring word "knife" was picked out of the blur of sound with expressionist intensity until the word was like the thrust of a knife in her mind. That was unprecedented and off camera. On camera, the Czechoslovakian Ondra was pretty and appealing, but her English was wretched. So Hitch had Joan Barry, fluent and accomplished, standing off camera saying the lines as Ondra fluttered her lips

Thirty years later, as *Psycho* was being made, Hitchcock's devoted crew were uneasy. Many of them were from the television unit he had assembled in the 1950s for *The Alfred Hitchcock Hour*. Now they were making a feature film, but one that departed from Hitch's own norms in going back to black-and-white. A crew on a film hardly knows what's in the director's mind. He doesn't have time to tell them, and he may not be clear himself. The crew see fragments of a picture coming to uncertain life. Long before the "auteur" theory, crews looked at directors in the way shipboard life relies on the wisdom of the captain. They want to have someone in charge, just to hold off the chaos that frequently threatens a picture.

So the crew on *Psycho* felt this project was a departure for their boss. They knew that what had started out as a Paramount picture ended up being done at Universal. There were rumors that that was because original bosses flinched at the tastelessness of the project. There were worries that the whole thing was not going to work, that it might seem ridiculous and grotesque. Then one day the composer Bernard Herrmann appeared with a rough track of his first attempts at a score for *Psycho.* Herrmann was an illustrious maverick, a difficult collaborator sometimes, but he had composed the scores for *Citizen Kane, On Dangerous Ground, Vertigo,* and *North by Northwest,* among others. He played what he was planning for *Psycho* (of course, he had had many consultations with Hitchcock) and the mood on set changed. The music explained that unique film to the doubters. The tastelessness was lifted up to the level of a grim, piercing opera. The music was a sky in which this daring picture could fly.

All of which sounds like a happy resolution, as if any problematic film could be tidied up and made sweet with a generous application of music, like syrup being poured on old pancakes. Alas, there are too many pictures where that policy seems to have been followed, and where music sinks to the level of muzak. Sometimes music is stripped in and out, like cheap carpeting. On *Chinatown,* shortly before the film was released, various parties felt Phillip Lambro's score was inadequate. The producer, Robert Evans, was never one to shirk bold action. He turned to another composer, Jerry Goldsmith, and gave him ten days to write a fresh score. The result is famous, moody, wistful, fatalistic, and romantic. Those words are only gestures toward an adequate description, but you may be humming the opening refrain to *Chinatown* as you read.

Music is one part of the story. In the shower sequence from *Psycho,* it's possible to distinguish many other sound elements: the roar of the running water; the screams of Marion Crane (though it is not clear whether Janet Leigh is doing the screaming); the faint but unmistakable sounds of a knife hacking at flesh (accomplished with a water melon); the violent rise and fall of the music, to suggest the knife thrusts as well as the terror; and, I think, a level at which the music and the screams are blended electronically.

Those strands of sound have been balanced and mixed in one married sound track, but notice how different interests are served by the marriage: the sounds of water, of a knife hacking, and of screams might be said to be live sound from an actual event. But the music is far more complicated. Is it Marion's point of view, or Norman's? Is it us being told how to be afraid? Or is it Hitchcock the ringmaster stoking up the atmosphere, because we might not be fully upset without it? Is it even some neutral, observing force—we could call it fate—that is witnessing this hideous incident? Is it the spirit of fear that lives in old motels at night? Is it another "once upon a time"? That last question is relevant because music goes all through the film, and covers several different characters, or scenes, where no one is present. Is the music even akin to a narrative tone, like the rhythm in a prose narrative?

When Goldsmith's music starts up on *Chinatown,* before a character has appeared, let alone spoken, does it not represent the mood and sadness of the story to come, a flavor of Los Angeles in 1937, or 1937 as viewed and felt from 1974, nostalgia for the noir spirit? For surely that music is signaling the emotional terrain of the film, and clearing its throat as if to say, Now, let me tell you a sad story. . . . Yet the mournful chords of *Chinatown*'s opening music are a long way from the bawdy humor of its first scene.

Nothing is said in the shower scene in *Psycho,* beyond screaming, but it's instructive to consider how many levels of voice there are in the film. There is the off-camera sound of "mother" berating Norman, a voice in the air, not attached to a person, but oddly echoing and disturbing. There is the closing voice of the mother noting how she is not going to kill that fly—and I don't think it is the voice used earlier. (Paul Jasmin and Virginia Gregg contributed to these personae.) There are the voices Marion hears during her drive north, into the night and the rain, the voices of possible pursuit and punishment. There are even the voices of the characters talking together. Anthony Perkins and Janet Leigh make a subtle and touching supper scene, oddly gentle and calming, before the outburst of the shower. They sound hushed, alone together; it feels like night. These voices are essential to the drama, and (as noted) Norman's is the first kind voice after a series of nagging, grating speakers. In the voice itself, in the quality of its talk, and in the intimate way it is recorded, Norman seems to be a rescuer, a friend, even a lover. Anthony Perkins has the wrong voice for a psychopath—which only shows how tricky those guys can be.

When I talk of the way *Psycho* is recorded I am touching upon a wealth of craft more easily understood in practice than described. But voices in a movie need to be placed: they can be in a field, a dining room, in a secret place shared with another person, in the course of a kiss, on the edge of madness, inside the speaker's head, or in a cave of loneliness. The voice can be surrounded by rebarbative metal surfaces, in an empty room, or in a velvet alcove. More than that, it can offer an attitude to the story. Thus, Carol Reed's voice-over at the start of *The Third Man* is brisk, cynical, worldly, and in an open space; George Sanders's narrative as Addison DeWitt in *All About Eve* is knowing, insinuating, gossipy, snide, and actorly—and in a private room; and in *The Magnificent Ambersons,* Orson Welles's narrative is fond, amused, and omniscient yet ready for a kind of tragedy that knowledge cannot prevent. It could be a voice looking into a dying fire late at night. Reed has been recorded in a studio without undue fuss or care; Sanders has been treated with DeWitt's odd mixture of self-love and self-loathing; and Welles's narrator comes from the heart of his own rosebud. Of those three, Welles knew and cared the most about sound. He had been raised in radio. He had won his chance at a movie because of the daring and cheek behind his 1938 broadcast of *The War of the Worlds.*

Before Welles, no movie director had had such aptitude for sound, or such experience with its potential for trickery. Sound was still novel in 1938 (the era of the Mercury Theatre on the Air). When it came to the movies, first in 1927, it was so laborious, so difficult, and so limited in its achievements that there were ample reasons to disapprove of it. Moreover, the accident of history meant that the enormous investment required to equip movie studios and then the theaters for sound coincided with the impact of the Depression. The audience shrank drastically as new investment was needed. Many film practitioners lamented the loss of purity and eloquence that the silent film had reached. But nothing impeded public appetite for the new asset.

Early sound encumbered the camera. It had to be put in a soundproof box, so it could not move as freely as it had done in *Sunrise,* say. A number of movie stars discovered that they could not sound American, fluent, or as beautiful as their faces. Garbo is a charismatic screen personality enhanced by speech—but she possessed and learned to develop a seductive deep voice that suited her face. In addition, she rarely said too much. John Gilbert was less lucky: he sounded more like Chaplin than Ronald Colman. This is the material of a film like *Singin' in the Rain,* where Debbie Reynolds's character talks sweet to replace the wretched voice of the silent star played by Jean Hagen. That film treats the transition as comic, but it was tragic, too.

Aesthetically and technically, a principle was revealed in these maneuvers. The audience loved sound for a variety of reasons: for songs and music; for the gunfire in the gangster films of the new age; for the sepulchral groans and howls of Bela Lugosi and Boris Karloff in the horror films that set in with *Dracula* and *Frankenstein.* The singing movie star was on his and her way: Bing Crosby, Jeanette MacDonald, Maurice Chevalier, and even Dietrich, who sings in *Morocco* and then kicks sexual expectation forward a decade or so with the kiss she bestows on a pretty girl in the audience. That kiss occurs in a suspenseful hesitation that signaled another bonus with sound: at last people could be quiet, thoughtful, or inward. The locus of acting had shifted from pantomime to being. That seemed like naturalism, the way people wondered in real life, so sound seemed to complete the realistic capacity of film—the lifelike illusion.

Because they were technologically separate, voice and face did not have to fit. From speed or penury, or just because it amused him, on several later films Orson Welles used his own voice to dub in lines for other actors. You can regard that as a mischievous habit, but it may have deeper meaning. In *Kane*, the disappointed husband takes over Jed Leland's negative review of Susan Kane in her night at the opera, and completes it, with venom. On *The Exorcist*, as the child Regan's head revolves and she curses everything in sight while projectile vomiting, director William Friedkin had Mercedes McCambridge do the child's satanic voice. The result is shattering, even if Friedkin was unkind enough to deny McCambridge a credit—perhaps he wanted the otherworldliness of the voice to prevail. There is a legend that there is something of Debra Winger in the voice of E.T. Jack Hawkins was operated on for throat cancer in 1966, and for the last seven years of his career he mimed while other actors dubbed in his voice.

Those anecdotes only scratch the surface. In so many countries where subtitling is reckoned to be a deterrent to audiences, all the dialogue is dubbed. Sometimes this is done with great skill so that a voice actor may be a great star in Spain or Italy for several decades. But if we treasure real voices—if we would be inclined to place that attribute very high in any estimate of John Wayne, Margaret Sullavan, James Cagney, Barbara Stanwyck, Jeanne Moreau, or Jean-Paul Belmondo—then dubbing is an alteration of human nature, and one that is still taken for granted.

Dubbing, or looping, is also a way of rewriting, or heightening films. Dialogue can be recorded at the moment of shooting, but there are so many factors that can make that original sound quality less than perfect. So wild tracks are a source of guidance in postproduction, and a preparation for the careful building of the sound track later. That begins with the dialogue, where the players come to a sophisticated sound studio and record the words in time with their own moving lips—

unless the picture needs to alter its dialogue for some story reason: then the sharp-eyed viewer may notice that the picture goes out of synch for a moment or two. Most of the time is spent getting the actors to deliver their best reading, or acting, of the dialogue, and to give their voice the proper aural placement.

In the early years of sound, the talk was uniform and restricted. It seemed to be emerging from too much white noise or through a mesh of interactive brushes. You could hear the furtive noises of a studio and sometimes the bumps of filmmaking. Nowadays, we expect not just high fidelity (being able to hear what is said) but the ideal aural-emotional context for the words. That means telling indoors from the open air, knowing the size of the room, or the emotional scale of the action, and gauging the various kinds of room tone or supernatural presence in the sound. In the films of David Lynch—in *Blue Velvet* and *Mulholland Dr.*—rooms and corridors have their sound signature. On top of, or beneath that, there may be a hum or a grind that can hardly be translated into words, but which surely affects our response to what is going on. Some creature or machine is breathing.

Once upon a time, sound was credited to a recordist, but now it has its designers, as befits a new kind of décor. Presence or effects are not new. But the sophistication in recording technology has made great progress—so long as the various theaters, our television sets, or our computers can match it. I have been present at sound mixes in the best studios in America and heard variations in aural pressure or stealthy presence that I have never heard again in regular commercial outlets. Today a sound designer wants to know whether the wind required in a film is a mounting storm in Mongolia, the tropic winds in

Hawaii, or the nagging Santa Ana of mental disorder. It may be real wind recorded by a field unit, or it may be an actor blowing into a box.

You never know what will work—but you know not to trust the real thing. Sound effects are negotiable items—like the sound of Cary Grant's battered top hat thumping against Katharine Hepburn's silky bottom in *Bringing Up Baby* to protect her exposed panties from view and humiliation. Was that recorded on set, or was it a Hawksian joke discovered later in bursting a small paper bag? A sound designer has an ear for nature and real life, of course, but he does not rely on that. He listens as carefully as the spectator must learn to do.

In 1982, Robert Towne wrote and directed a film, *Personal Best,* in which two Olympic-caliber athletes (played by Mariel Hemingway and Patrice Townsend) become lovers. The film would have many sequences of the women running, and Towne was anxious to get the right sound of feet on the track. Recording units were sent here and there to running tracks in Oregon and California, but it was not easy to record a runner running. When the microphone moved, the sound level fluctuated. Towne was close to giving up on his idea of perfection when one day, in the postproduction studio, someone dropped a full reel of 35 mm film. The coils of film went flap-flap-flap. It was the sound the team had been looking for, and because the reel of film was stationary, each flap was like another. In other words, it was running as it sounded to a runner. No one claimed that it sounded precisely like running. But it worked on the sound track. It sounded right.

Yet sometimes sounding wrong is right. At a critical juncture in *The Godfather,* Michael Corleone goes to meet his enemies, Sollozzo and McCluskey, in a neighborhood Italian restaurant.

They have come close to murdering Michael's father, Vito, and the son wants vengeance. The Corleone family have contrived to hide a loaded gun in the lavatory cistern at the restaurant. It is a pleasant place, with a small group of diners. "Try the veal," says Sollozzo. "It's the best in town." Perhaps, but surely that kind of modest yet distinguished restaurant would not tolerate the periodic din of a subway train running just below it? Yet as Michael emerges from the lavatory and kills his enemies, the noise of the train rises by a factor of three or four. The loco now seems to be hurtling through the room. This is the device of the sound designer Walter Murch (he was credited as post-production consultant), and you can argue, reasonably, that the sound of the train is a measure of Michael's trepidation and our suspense. Spelled out like that, the device can seem calculating. But it worked in 1972. Today? Perhaps it begins to seem more cold-blooded, but that is a sign of how even the best films can become dated. And maybe we have seen *The Godfather* too many times—it is like a club for which we want to keep up our membership.

What matters in this example is the evidence that sound can be taken out of all proportion to make a uniquely cinematic effect, but one that is no more fanciful than a camera and its crew being there in the restaurant unnoticed, while a musical score plays in the air. I think it's clear that a restaurant as reputable as this one, and favored by these people, would not play music to encourage its diners to hurry—unless they had that much propensity for melodrama. That's where the subway train is inseparable from the music. (Of course, the restaurant will change after the double hit.)

The subway is a huge intrusion, but sound effects can be far smaller. Robert Bresson's *A Man Escaped* concerns a French

Resistance agent, Fontaine, who has been captured by the Gestapo. While anticipating torture or execution, he thinks of getting free. So he fashions a spoon to dig at crumbling masonry, and he has to listen for the muffled sounds of prison life that warn of guards. To hear the film and to share the man's plight is to become sensitive to all these small scraping noises. And it is not just elation, but aesthetic triumph, that when he is free at last the small noises are replaced by Mozart's Great Mass in C Minor.

Music was never too far from movies. Often, when emotional scenes were being shot, a silent production would have a violinist on set, or a trio, to set up a fitting mood for the actors. When we look at silent pictures, it is helpful to feel that some of the players are ecstatic or tormented in line with music they are hearing. Music, dance, and singing are some of the ways in which many people can lose their inhibitions. It may also account for the several set expressions of silent screen acting—beseeching, demanding, reacting, needing—a series of markedly outward signals, as opposed to the more inward acting that came when talking actors felt less pressing need to carry the message or spell out the action of a film.

That on-set music might be reproduced in theaters where a piano, an organ, a string quartet, or even a full orchestra played "suitable" or encouraging music for the film. If you've ever had the chance to watch a film with a veteran accompanist, someone who worked in the silent era, you will know that such practitioners possessed a repertoire of set-up tunes, emotional triggers, and standard refrains that covered most ordinary actions—walking, running, running away, pursuing, charging, riding to the rescue. It was a scheme that soon grew limited. A few films had composed scores—Hugo Riesenfeld wrote an orchestral score for *Sunrise,* for instance—but that was an expense that could not be borne by a film as it traveled the country. Moreover, this accompaniment was visible, energetic, like performers in a play. The toiling musicians could not help but detract from the magic of a musical score that arose in the air without labor or strain, and was as essential and inexplicable as the light show itself. Among many other things, music on the sound track helped us believe we were alone with the miracle, with music unchosen by us, unbidden, but seeming like the natural companion to the actors and the action.

As on *Chinatown,* the people in charge of a film are at pains to get the music "right." It's easy therefore to assume that they have been successful; Max Steiner's music for *Gone With the Wind* is as famous as the film, and redolent of movies in that era before the Second World War. In *Laura,* the picture is streamlined by David Raksin's lush theme which is now known as "Laura"—it was given lyrics later on by Johnny Mercer and it became a hit song. But suppose that in the film of *Laura* the song that kept playing had been "Long Ago (and Far Away)," by Jerome Kern. That was another 1944 song and it was written for the picture *Cover Girl,* where Rita Hayworth sang it to Gene Kelly. But it only seemed to be Hayworth. That fabulous dancer had a poor voice so she mimed to a recording by Martha Mears. But "Long Ago" would work in *Laura,* because both songs are written on the idea of a lost love or an occasion from the past.

As for Steiner's music for *Gone With the Wind,* it may be immortal, but why don't you play some parts of the film to the accompaniment of, say, Franz Waxman's music for *A Place in the Sun,* the slow movement from Mahler's Fifth Symphony, or even Louis Armstrong's "Potato Head Blues"?

That goes too far? I'm sure you're right. Still, you may be surprised and tickled at how well "Long Ago" and the Waxman work. And when the complacent Selznick era's views of black folks are put beside the blazing lyricism of Louis and the Hot Seven (1927), we have a history lesson on our plate. These wayward alternatives are not unhelpful. Edgar Ulmer's *Detour* (1945), a raffish noir classic, includes the song "I Can't Believe That You're in Love with Me" (sung as it happens by Martha Mears), as well as some selections from Chopin. But try that macabre, ultra-economical movie about loathing and chance with Erik Satie's *Gymnopédies* (written in 1888), a sparse piece for lonely piano. The result is stunning, and somehow the trashy jewel of a film becomes an enigmatic, existential parable. How can such things be? The answer (and I will not claim that the method is unfailing) is that there is a natural affair (it's not a marriage—the illicit lurks) between the movies and music that has its roots in the word "melodrama."

So you were ready to believe that film is one great ocean of visual material that requires the most careful attention? You thought it is about watching? But sound is a second ocean, hiding in the first.

I have left till last the thing announced in "the talkies"— human voices communing, snarling, or falling in love (if it's a Hawks film, *His Girl Friday* or *To Have and Have Not,* it's all three). It's still the case that some sound films take pride in doing without talk—as if an old purity has been regained. So critics and scholars honor the long silent robbery in *Rififi,* and they enjoy stories of John Ford ripping pages of fussy talk out of his scripts, or Clint Eastwood or Steve McQueen refusing a line because they reckon they can carry it in their faces.

Those are fine moments, deserving of recognition. But be

wary if film culture and cinephilia ever seem to be hostile to talk for the sake of hostility, and in the cause of grim silence. One of my favorite stills is of Brando, Duvall, and Caan on the set of *The Godfather*. All seems normal, but Duvall wears a tabard-length white sheet on which Brando's lines are written out in capitals. So Brando is staring forward at Duvall's navel—and giving a great performance. Talk is rapture, and it is everyday: it is the insane linguistics of Abbott and Costello's "Who's on First?" and the mounting folly of Groucho talking to Chico—antipathy enough to make us wonder why the Marx Brothers never became a gang to rival *Bonnie and Clyde*. Nearly as much as a modern talksmith, Aaron Sorkin, I love the times in Hawks's pictures when Bogart and Bacall, or Grant and Hepburn, fence with words. Whatever its moody aura of Los Angeles, with guns and cars and dames, *The Big Sleep* is our most audacious screwball comedy, with the greatest of telephone scenes. But don't let those estimates put you off *The Lady Eve* and *Sullivan's Travels*, *Midnight* and *My Man Godfrey*, or even *To Have and Have Not*, in which the flag of the Free French comes down in favor of innuendo and wisecracks. To hear Rudy Vallee talk in *The Palm Beach Story* is to be close to heaven. To hear the chill politeness of Catherine Deneuve in *Belle de Jour* is to be there. What a couple she and Vallee would make.

After all, talk has the chance of intelligence, wit, and the attempt to speak to people. With those hopes, talk can be the surest way of handling the opposite sexes. In the verbal overdrive of Abraham Polonsky's *Force of Evil*, John Garfield's crooked lawyer could be speaking blank verse. I ache whenever the doomed but ardent voice of James Mason reaches up toward hope, whether as Humbert in *Lolita* or Johnny in *Odd*

Man Out. Quentin Tarantino is so besotted with movie talk that it often obscures his ignorance of life. I am happy to have talk brief and pungent, and many of us squirm at the spread of "small talk" about 1.2 seconds after it begins. In general, the more pained, sincere, and life-affirming a speech in a film the shorter time it will endure. I groan at Paul Muni getting ready to save the world, and I despair over the sermons in the films of Stanley Kramer, Frank Capra, and John Cassavetes. I never wanted to be among the people Ma Joad embraces at the end of *The Grapes of Wrath,* but I could listen forever to Jimmy Stewart and Margaret Sullavan bickering in *The Shop Around the Corner.* The only hope for a lasting relationship is argument, misunderstanding, and the ensuing comedy.

There is no sure recipe for talk, beyond having writers and actors and listeners who can do it. That means people who believe in it, who appreciate tone of voice, hesitation, and the great collection of sounds that go with talk—the sighs, the grunts, the gasps, the giggles, the groans. Do you still hear the orchestra of nonverbal sounds uttered by Timothy Spall's *Mr. Turner*? All of which can come down to something as simple and infinite as *The Lady Eve* and Stanwyck murmuring thank you to Henry Fonda when he draws down the hem of her dress after it has risen unaccountably in the warmth of their kissing.

Have you ever listened properly to a kiss?

10

WHAT IS A STORY,
AND DOES IT MATTER?

Tell me a story," we beg as children, while wanting so many other things. Story will put off sleep (or extinction), and the child's organism hardly trusts the habit of waking yet. It means relationship with a storyteller: being read to is the template of every intimacy in life. Moreover, it was in rising to the challenge of story that movie went from being a craze to a universal entertainment, and an art form. Still, film is curious: the storyteller may fall asleep before the child, but movie is story or a continuity that carries on without us. It is time itself, and time does not have to be organized, until we insist on it.

A film show runs mechanically; that is part of its charm, but the thrill is faintly sinister, too. (It *would* carry on without us.) If an actress onstage halts in the middle of a speech from *Electra,* say, because she can't continue, then that performance and its play stop. All of which leaves story in an intriguing but uncertain position in a medium that has its own momentum and continuity. We are there to watch and we are likely to watch wherever that imperative takes us. So sometimes we end up watching things we might never have chosen. Yet still we cling to this idea—tell me a story, because a story can avert or deny the most frightening thing of all, the abyss, the great hole of insignificance, and the dread that we have no story.

Consider *All Is Lost* (2013), where Robert Redford is alone in a small boat in the Pacific. This is easily presented as a story: it has an abrupt start and that almost demands a settling answer. A man in his mid-seventies wakes up alone on his yacht one morning, 1,700 miles from Sumatra. He has felt a great bump, and now there is seawater slapping around in his cabin. While he slept his yacht has been struck by a container that must have slipped off some cargo ship. The container is brick red in color and maybe sixty feet long. It is a bizarre new monster of the deep, and it is leaking running shoes into the Pacific from the point of impact. The damage to the yacht is greater. There is a gash in its side so large that as and when the seas turn rough the boat will take on too much water to stay afloat. The same impact has destroyed the yachtsman's means of communication. (That might happen, though experienced yachtsmen think it fanciful; but this story *requires* his isolation—that's what keeps us there.)

Anyone seeing the film calls the man "Redford"—he is the only actor in the picture and he is there all the time. He never acquires a fictional name; when the credits roll at the end of the film he is referred to as "Our Man." That's touching and suggestive. It's not quite "our hero," but it assumes some allegiance on our part, and some exemplary status on his. As if

All Is Lost is a fable, "Our Man" means he represents us. Still, we know nothing about him. Is he taking part in a round-the-world, single-handed race such as was popular in the sixties and seventies? There is no sign of it. Is he a dying man who has taken on a last challenge? Is he seeking to escape an impossible domestic situation? Has his wife died, or did he leave her for a younger woman who then dropped him? Has a child died or disowned Our Man? We are given no clue for exploring these possibilities, though at the outset we hear his voice compose a message saying he tried his best—to survive, and to live, too. It's not clear whether this message—he will put it in a bottle and send it off—is for his own dear ones, or for the world. Our Man has only a vague sense of us and who we might be, except that if he is a story then we are the ones to whom it is being told. We're looking at him, and we're the only ones close to "there."

He tries unsuccessfully to raise a radio operator on his broken equipment and later he will cry out at the fates. As written and directed by J. C. Chandor, the film does not succumb to an interior monologue, to panic, or to a crack-up. Our man wants to survive; he does everything he can think of, but there is something stoic and resigned in his silence. As his yacht founders, he goes to the emergency raft. He tries to attract attention. There is a moment when a fully loaded container ship passes him in broad daylight, but it has no lookouts and no one to hear his cries. The ship is from a ghost fleet, an ominous reminder of that other container vessel that lost the red rogue that struck him. It is also a metaphor for the blind corporate momentum that cannot notice the individual in need of help.

There is a fearsome storm, and we believe in Our Man being

tossed about in the shaking yacht. But the storm is not entirely elemental. A camera keeps filming it and we understand that if Redford the actor had had to beg for rest it would have been granted. The night storm scenes are done in a tank where the waves can be manipulated. The illusion of ordeal survives, yet we know this is a contrivance. And because Our Man is so alone, that peril is all the more nominal. This has many resemblances to a desperate, tense story, yet it is as naked and theoretical as a diagram in the proving of a theorem. So many films have "desperate" situations, but several hundred people and a completion bond are keeping it under control. Yet *All Is Lost* makes us believe (while leaving us in doubt).

That's where the title becomes important. It is an assertion that seems to say that the end is known before we begin, so that conventional suspense should be abandoned. It's a title that applies to Our Man and his yacht, yet it is more resonant—could this even refer to the twenty-first-century fear that, in more ways than we can begin to deal with, our civilization is edging toward demise? As we watch the film, and participate in its ordeal, the title seems foreboding. The inquisitive part of us wonders, How are "they" going to end this film? After all, they started it, and who embarks on a story without some thought of an ending? Did Redford come on board to die? Must this film be a downer, or will it be clever enough to find offsetting sources of romance and sentiment such as turned *Titanic* into a popular success? Can Our Man conjure up a Girl Friday? *All Is Lost* does not feel extravagant, but it does have a movie star in a big situation. It is said to have cost only $10 million, which means that Redford took little money up front. Still, it was a mainstream film, an old-fashioned adventure picture, with a chance at Oscars. So the question of how to end the picture is there from the start. It can't go on forever; yet it can't simply stop. We need a signal to go home.

I suspect there were several endings in J. C. Chandor's head. (Someday, we will want films that show the alternate endings, and that lay out script directions not taken.) There could be a breathtaking, last-minute rescue. The life raft might be cast upon a desert island where Girl Friday is making tea and sympathy. God could intervene. The film could acquire the fierce assistance of a Bengal tiger named Richard Parker. Or Our Man may drown or go crazy from lack of water, roasting in the sun—the way people do perish in extremis. He might give up the ghost and slip into the water, like Captain Oates leaving Scott's camp for "a walk" on the way back from the South Pole in 1912.

I think this is what happens. Night falls. Our Man sees a light in the distance that must be another vessel. He begins to burn whatever he has to attract attention. The light comes toward him. Will it arrive in time? Will it be another ship? Is it a mirage? At the moment of crisis, in one swift shot an arm reaches out to grasp Our Man as he founders. Black out. End of film. Has he been saved, or has he died? Whose arm was that? And does one end exclude the other? Imagine *All Is Lost* as a film by Robert Bresson, and the ambiguity of the ending could be a moment of spiritual exultation. In fact, music builds towards the end of *All Is Lost,* and I fear that is the greatest weakness in the film. But it takes wisdom in a director to know when to use Mozart, Louis Armstrong, or silence.

J. C. Chandor is a young American filmmaker. He delivered the sickening emptiness at the end of his first film, *Margin Call.* He delivered the very subtle and absorbing *A Most Violent Year.* He knew he was making a Robert Redford picture here and he was likely at ease with the unspoken assumption that Redford comes out of his films well, though not always in victory. He is about to be shot to pieces in *Butch Cassidy and the Sundance Kid*. He was compromised in *The Way We Were*. He is murdered in *The Chase*. But he has never been crushed or broken. He has never seemed rotten or dishonest. He has been able to think well of himself—and like other actors he may need that bonus. Chandor found a way of ending his picture with honor, or its mirror image, while leaving an intriguing openness.

So how do we follow a story without becoming story theorists, or would-be screenwriters? As Hilary Mantel said recently, "History is a set of skills rather than a narrative." Story is an ancient cultural form remade by the movies, as profound and misleading as the cult of happiness, everything working out for the best, and order standing firm. These motifs spring directly from an old picture business adage: If we don't send an audience away feeling good they may not come back. For decades, until well into the 1960s, movie storytelling was usually positive and always tidy. Without those faithful elements the show risked our dismay. *Citizen Kane* was a box-office failure (despite good reviews) because it did not pay off in the customary way. The search for the meaning of "Rosebud" nearly slipped into oblivion. It only worked if you were attentive enough to track the sled through the movie and share Kane's feeling of loss. Even then, you had no reason to feel Kane had ended well, or happily. He had died in exile from his own world, shut in his own head, and the movie had not made audiences care for him in any conventional way. Indeed, the picture felt as ambivalent toward him as most of his colleagues felt about Orson Welles. In going so deeply into the mind of a little boy tycoon, the film ended irresolute. It made us uncomfortable.

Story is often closely linked to comfort. "I'll tell you a story" is a parental promise, and the teller of the tale will look after us even if the story is frightening in parts. This is also the way the silly confusion of the romantic plots in Fred Astaire films are wiped aside in a final dance routine and a shower of applause. It is the way lovers are brought together, their last embrace rippling on the closing curtains. It is the way adventure heroes—from Tom Mix to James Bond, from Mickey Mouse to E.T.—overcome all enemies and leave the world in an orderly shape. More than just the clicking together of narrative elements in movies, this is the way for more than three decades a dozen stories a day on television ended with a cursory but doubt-free air of settlement and well-being, as emphatic as the assurances in the commercials that paid for the programs. Grant that his cop was shabby, vulgar, homely, and one-eyed, still Columbo—like Perry Mason or Jessica Fletcher in *Murder, She Wrote*—solved every case and outwitted every wrongdoer. These defenders of right were as trustworthy as Woodward and Bernstein in *All the President's Men*. That was Robert Redford again, saving America from corruption and wanting to believe that newspapers would protect the Constitution.

All the President's Men worked very cunningly: it had stars, noir suspense, a portrait of iniquity, and the thought that things were going to be OK, not the beginning of the end for newspapers. This optimism can be an American blindness after which exhaustive, critical inspection seems preferable, if less likely. Consider a contrasting movie, that of *Ida* (2013). We are in Poland in 1962. A young woman, Anna, is about to take her vows to become a nun. She had thought she was an orphan, cared for by the Church. But her Mother Superior tells her she has an aunt, and she must visit her before the decisive step of taking the vows.

The aunt, Wanda, has lost any faith in vows. She was a fierce Communist once. As a prosecutor she sent some people to their deaths. But she has lost that conviction. She is alone and growing older. She smokes and drinks and has a lot of careless, hopeless sex. She is a skeptic to her own chance of story. But she has narrative news for Anna—they are both Jewish, and Anna's parents were murdered in the war by Polish Catholics. So Wanda is like a grave test now: understand your past and your nature, she tells Anna—and see if you can still take your vows. After all, your true name is Ida.

The film of *Ida* is only eighty minutes. I won't spoil the ending for you, and saying that does admit that endings can be precious. But what promises to be a great test for Ida becomes as much of a rite of passage for Wanda. Enormous crimes are uncovered in the process, along with the downcast admission that the criminals were as human as the victims.

I spoke of indefatigable detectives on screen, and in story the viewers are detectives, too, at the foot of the screen. That's one reason why *Vertigo* is so instructive. James Stewart plays a police detective retired on account of his vertigo. A few years earlier Stewart had been the single-minded investigator who worked out the truth in *Rear Window*. In *Vertigo*, he makes a hash of the case; he brings about the death of the woman he has fallen in love with; and he lets the murderer escape. Was it that degree of failure that made *Vertigo* a flop, or was it because Hitchcock could find no way of telling the story without revealing its ending too early? Perhaps it was just a matter of time; in 1958 audiences wanted suspense that played fair. But by 2012, the analysis of tragedy in *Vertigo* was not just recognizable; it seemed necessary.

Into the 1960s, such conclusions became more common or

more respected. Michelangelo Antonioni's *L'Avventura* looks like the case of a missing woman who has vanished on a trip to an offshore island. But then interest in her disappearance fades away in what proves to be less a mystery story than a film about emotional forgetting and disloyalty. We never discover what happened to her. Antonioni loved such endings: *L'Eclisse, Blow-Up,* and even *The Passenger* end in a kind of hiatus. *Magnolia* ends like a flower: so many petals, some dying, some in bloom. It enjoys the wildness in life, hence its frogs. *McCabe & Mrs. Miller* has a heroic resolution in which the inept McCabe disposes of the three bad guys sent to kill him, but no one in the township has seen what he has done. He will be misunderstood again. In Scorsese's *Taxi Driver,* the fundamentally unfit Travis Bickle is still a cabbie in the city, no matter the slaughter he has caused or our doubts about his sanity. In *Chinatown,* one of the more unpleasant villains in American pictures, Noah Cross (John Huston), remains in charge of Los Angeles and guardian to the granddaughter who is actually his daughter. The detective, Jake Gittes (Jack Nicholson), is led away, on the point of breakdown, with the advice, "Forget it, Jake, it's Chinatown"—the system is too intricate and corrupt for him.

Television's surfeit of stories bred mockery and observations about there being only seven or nine story shapes in the entire history of fiction. Audiences caught these familiar rhythms and took story novelty less seriously. At the London National Film Theatre in the 1960s, there was a famous patron who sat on the end of a row and left a few minutes before the end of every film. She said she knew the way films worked well enough to feel closure coming and she resented the drab rites of explanation. The adroit Hitchcock was nearly defeated by the need to explain *Psycho* at the end, and that otherwise trembling film has a soporific passage where a psychiatrist (Simon Oakland) lets us go home with a necessary and cleansing understanding of this bizarre psychotic behavior. But then *Psycho* rallies with the last glimpse (and sound) of Norman and his mother not just reunited but impacted. So it ends on a gotcha.

The old narrow-minded emphasis on story and narrative surprise has given way to the reenactment of ritual, or dream. There has been a mood in some modern films that says life is never simply one story. It is more likely a collection of overlapping stories: thus the interest in anthology films, like *Nashville* and *Short Cuts* (by Robert Altman), *Boogie Nights* and *Magnolia* (by Paul Thomas Anderson), and Paul Haggis's *Third Person*. Those films seem truer to what we see around us, and they heed the realization that everyone feels he or she must be the center of the universe, and thus a star, when we are all nothing more than supporting actors surrounded by others.

There are also notable pictures that treat story less as a compelling object of attention than a climate of many passing moods. In *Providence,* with a novelist (John Gielgud) as a central character, Alain Resnais shows us a variety of scenes, all of which are more projections than definite actuality. In *That Obscure Object of Desire,* on impulse, Luis Buñuel decided to replace one absent actress (Maria Schneider) with two women to share the one part (Angela Molina and Carole Bouquet). But the man who lusts after this woman (Fernando Rey) cannot tell one actress from the other, so he is hopelessly confused when they veer off in bifurcated seductive modes. There's another level of reference in that film, for Rey's suave womanizer is plainly related to the Frenchman, Alain Charnier, in *The French Connection* (1971). Buñuel and Rey borrow the look of that character. But that wit is only one step in the realization that all along in movies many actors had been themselves and variants on their own archetype. So Christina Crawford's book on her adoptive mother, Joan Crawford—*Mommie Dearest*—and the film that came from it, are, consciously or not, anthologies of Crawford's career and the ever more hysterical emotional tyrants she played.

In *Céline and Julie Go Boating*, two young women become intrigued by what is happening in an elegant but rather mysterious house in Paris. When they gain entrance they see that an obscure melodrama is playing there in continuous performance: a story in which a child is menaced by three very mannered adults. Céline and Julie then realize that they may be able to intervene in that story and save the little girl. This is couched in terms of gentle comedy, with the events inside the house looking more and more movielike, but the attitude could as easily furnish a sinister story in which the oppressive weather of movie is going to drive people crazy. Examples of that darker tendency could include Andrei Tarkovsky's *Stalker* (1979), where men travel through a wasteland to the mythic Zone where desires are made into life, or *Pierrot le Fou*, where the female character (Anna Karina, until lately the wife of the film's director, Jean-Luc Godard) talks to the camera and the force behind it, and the fusion of betrayal in life and fiction is exhilarating but tragic.

In story, we were attached to the moral being of characters. This is the crux of the nineteenth-century novel in so many languages, and it carried over into movie for at least a hundred years. So we care about what will happen to Scarlett O'Hara, to Montgomery Clift in *A Place in the Sun*, to Marshall Will Kane in *High Noon*, to Bette Davis and Anne Baxter in *All About Eve*. It looks like an orthodoxy in which characters fought the good fight to overcome obstacles, to be themselves, and to find true love. But there were wild places in that uniform landscape. In *To Have and Have Not* (1944) and *The Big Sleep* (1946), a sardonic, blithe travesty is made of the wartime action genre and the detective story, and the films become just about anything Bogart and Bacall care to do. They may not have known it. Director Howard Hawks may not have been certain. But they are making a new kind of film, a satire on set conventions. This approach would hardly be dared again until Jean-Luc Godard's films of the early 1960s, which are casual, fond, but derisive remakes of Hollywood schemes.

But times keep changing. Anyone wondering how to watch a movie is nowadays often engaged in following what we call long-form television, serial versions of certain situations and characters that may run for several series. These shows are made on budgets and schedules that hark back to the factory system of Hollywood. They depend on good writing and fine character acting, and they tend to fix on groups of people who face dramatic crises but never quite settle them. That could end the series. I am thinking of shows like *The Sopranos, The Wire, Homeland, Big Love, The Hour, The Fall, Rubicon, Luck, Masters of Sex, Ray Donovan, Boardwalk Empire, Breaking Bad,* and *Peaky Blinders.* Some succeed better than others, or last much longer. But that success presents creative problems.

In the nature of dramatic writing, one creates a character to see what will happen to him or her—the matter of moral resolution has not vanished, even if it has receded. So from the outset Tony Soprano was a conventional New Jersey boss in organized crime beset with doubts. He needed a shrink. He had family problems and difficult children. He was in middle age. Walter White, from *Breaking Bad,* is a hardworking, luckless, high-school chemistry teacher with domestic problems, but still trying to get along with life—like 99 percent of his audience. Then he finds he has lung cancer and he is outraged that dedication and playing by the rules have failed him. So he will take life and the law into his own hands. He diverts his knowledge of chemistry to making drugs. And what will become of him?

The dramatist, or the creator of such a show, wants closure. He dreams of a finale full of corpses or a hero who has been redeemed. But the same person is also riding the monster of television success. It isn't just the immediate audience they get, or the sale of boxed sets. With enough seasons, these shows go into syndication—and *I Love Lucy* is still making money on that mechanism. So the dramatist wants it both ways: he wants tragic resolution (sometimes it's comic) but he wants the show to go on as long as life. Those feelings are shared by the actors whose salaries go up with a long run—so long as they are not killed off. It does not diminish the power or value of these series to be honest about the commercial pressures. But good shows can develop their own hysteria.

Homeland began in 2011, created by Alex Gansa and Howard Gordon (and derived from an Israeli show). The show depended on the character of Carrie Mathison, a brilliant CIA agent who was also bipolar, in need of constant medication, and frequently on the edge of breakdown. In the first season she became involved with Brody (Damian Lewis), a prisoner returned from Iraq and possibly a terrorist agent. Carrie had to investigate him; but she also fell in love with him. Immediately, this stretched credibility. We like to think that the CIA is shy of employing bipolar victims who fall for their targets. Equally, it was far-fetched that under so much suspicion Brody would rise to elected office and the chance of a vice-presidential nomination. Still, the first season climaxed in espionage suspense and a tortured love situation with Carrie in hospital and shock therapy. Claire Danes gave a performance that had no superior on film and television in its time. She was so good she overcame fears of implausibility. She won awards and made many of us feel that we had never seen the bipolar condition so well handled. Which is not the same as watching a bipolar patient in anguish.

Then there was a second season, in which more or less the same things happened again, but suspending disbelief was that much greater a test.

And a third season, in which . . . Well, the people behind the show (and Danes was by then a producer) seemed to realize that a far-fetched situation was on the brink of nonsense. So Saul (Mandy Patinkin), the acting head of the CIA, dished Carrie at a congressional hearing. He admitted that she was unstable and unreliable. She was taken off duty and sent back to hospital. In one episode her hard life in recovery was paralleled with Brody's being held captive in a South American country by terrorists. And then *Homeland* came clean: Carrie now was *pretending* to be bipolar and at the end of her tether. This was part of a plot hatched by her and Saul to make Carrie available for overtures from Iranian intelligence and to lure them out into the open. So the actress was playing an actress.

What had happened with *Homeland* was story being sacrificed to commercial appetite (like the start time of a ballgame being moved to satisfy television schedules). The twists of plot invention had bigger pitfalls ahead. In season 3, Brody was executed, and Carrie discovered she was pregnant. What next? Season 4 wanted to press on with foreign intrigue and suspense, so it reckoned to send Carrie to a posting in Istanbul or Pakistan. But could her baby go with her? Well, scenarists must have felt a babe would get in the way (they had dropped Brody's family already), so the kid was left at home with Carrie's sister.

I reached my limit. (It left me more aware of the teasing delicacy with which David Chase had ended *The Sopranos* on a kind of pregnant vacancy.) I could go along with a bipolar woman given special trust by the CIA. I bought her love affair with a man who may be a terrorist: detectives screw up. And I liked the raw humanity Claire Danes brought to the role. But when the baby got dumped, I gave up on the show.

11

WHO MAKES THESE MOVIES?

I wanted to hug Lassie, to be in the same room as Gary Cooper, and to meet a projectionist. The miracle of the movies has always made us ask, Who did this? So in talking to you about how to watch a movie, the question of the who is important, at the level of authorship, and ownership. And remember that it's a truism in the business that *we* own the movies. You can hear producers and studios say that with touching piety, and mercenary stupidity. But their self-pity does lament the vagaries of the process: they put three years and $150 million into the works, and then on a Friday they face the truth. The public thinks it's junk. They walk away and never tell a friend to try it.

In the nicest way in the world, I have rubbed shoulders with vivid men and women doing fine work in picture production to whom one would not readily speak of "moral being" or "ontological validity." It's not that they didn't have access to those things, like a tuxedo for red carpet occasions. But philosophical self-advertising has been looked at askance in show business. It gets in the way of necessary egotism and the attitude (derived from the young Alexander Korda) that to make it in Hollywood you need to follow these blunt but enticing guidelines: move into the best hotels; frequent the most expensive restaurants; be seen with the most beautiful people in the most noble cars; charge everything; and tip lavishly. Then wait for offers. Hollywood has the best gallows humor about itself, if only to get in ahead of the scolds.

Don't tell the people there that Hollywood hardly exists now. That atmosphere lingers, not so much in the movies as in the contracts (as long as most scripts, and more carefully studied) and in the riot of Internet gossip. A lot of picture people are living in the past, their safest place. Moreover, there is another sound principle in the abandoned city: don't describe movies in language that would be incomprehensible to the people who made the pictures. But that can be hard. In the late 1950s, as the young writers on *Cahiers du Cinéma* and *Positif* hailed and reclaimed American directors who had felt lucky if they found work, they sometimes launched themselves on immense, flowery, and academic descriptions of films like *Detour, They Live by Night, Angel Face,* and *Run of the Arrow.* The makers of those excellent films might be flabbergasted and breathless at the questions. So sometimes they said "I guess so" to assertive and very flattering statements that had run on for a paragraph. The pattern became comic and touching in the celebratory interviews run in those magazines.

The first time I met Nicholas Ray was at Dartmouth College. He was a day out of Sloan-Kettering, where he had had operations for cancer. He was sixty-six but in his gauntness he seemed older. He was in very bad shape, not helped by having to make the small-plane flight from New York to the West Lebanon airport, the gateway to Dartmouth. The next morning I tried to get him to eat a small plate of scrambled eggs. This was encouraged by the presence of Susan, his fourth wife, a great believer in Nick, but someone who had learned dark truths along the way.

Nick Ray had made this trip for the modest fee that Dartmouth would pay him for appearing before the students. I suppose that might have been a warning: Ray was old before his time, frail, unsteady, not always coherent, ragged but handsome, with a black patch on one eye. The parents of those students could have surmised that Ray was the worst possible example, but it is my experience that film students—experts in the visual—see what they want to see.

I was in the same predicament and not much older than my students. I had admired Nicholas Ray since my youth: his *Rebel Without a Cause, In a Lonely Place, They Live by Night, Bitter Victory*—the titles themselves spoke to his desperate but romantic existentialism. So I talked to Nick in earnestness, and even love. I told him what he had meant to some of us. I reveled in the beauty of his pictures. I believed (I still do) that I was in the presence of a flawed genius and a wrecked man. Susan must have noticed this. I'm sure she had seen similar meetings in the time she had been with him. So, quietly, she came up to me, thanked me for being good for Nick, but cautioned me. "On no account," she said, "give him any money. He'll throw it away on drugs and gambling before morning." This was said with bleak kindness, like Gloria Grahame talking in *In a Lonely Place* about the difficulty of trust and love in Hollywood, and that great romanticization of self-destruction.

That meeting at Dartmouth was in 1978, I think, and *In a Lonely Place* was made in 1950. But Nick Ray was a battered icon, the visionary director who had stayed true to his unruly self and suffered for it. He had a persistent following who revered his independence as an artist and a film director and who looked upon his fallen status, his dire health, his history of family wreckage, his professional isolation, and his need for money as the signs of ontological validity. The truth was more complicated. John Houseman, the producer who had nursed Nick through his debut, *They Live by Night,* saw a man in turmoil, a spreader of human damage, a womanizer who was possibly a closet homosexual, and someone who never lost the passionate but incoherent hope that movies might be made by Baudelaire, Van Gogh, and Mahler—so long as they had a John Houseman to run interference. (Once upon a time, Houseman had served the same function for Orson Welles, and you can argue that Welles was never as organized after he threw Houseman out.)

So, the question arises, and it is one that every person who wants to know how to watch a movie asks—who makes these movies? J. C. Chandor has said that *All Is Lost* could not have been made without Robert Redford. Who else at that age could be so athletic, act without words, and help bank its modest budget? In his turn, Redford insisted that it was J.C.'s film as an idea, a story, and a work of cinema. I think I would say that Agata Trzebuchowska and Agata Kulesza were even more crucial to *Ida.* The way Pawel Pawlikowski made that film is driven by their two faces. Yet he grasped the drive, and I'm sure that other actresses—Polish or whatever—could have done very well in the roles. Better? Why bother to ask when we have such achievement?

So if you want to know who made a film, you can read the credits. But that's a wearying task now. That National Film Theatre escapee I mentioned could be home and making tea with you still in the dark processing the crawling roll of credits, in which we learn who trained the dogs, who negotiated the completion bond (though the exact and delicate circumstances of that evening are still in the dark), who drove whom to the set every morning. You can be put into a comatose state by this amount of information so that you might not recall there *were no dogs in the film*—but still trainers were credited. "Oh sure," you learn later, "they cut the dogs. In fact, I believe they sold the dog footage to another picture."

The credits on motion pictures have never been known for reliability. They are assertions in a business crowded out with self-promotion. They are gestures of ownership, profit participation, or guaranteed legal rights thanks to the negotiated stances of guilds and unions. There are even people who have been at pains to keep their names *off* films. Irving Thalberg's name appears on a film very seldom, yet we know he was a decisive executive who touched most Metro-Goldwyn-Mayer films between 1924 and 1936, for good and ill. By contrast, Jack Warner was happy to have his name on pictures, even those he'd barely heard of. One can mock that as self-importance, but most people who worked at Warners believed that Jack's power and say-so were crucial—also for good and ill. So many of our most beloved movies, waving the flag of great star presences, were the dream of moguls who owned the company. And America is very big on ownership—it can come close to art itself in a society where increasingly art comes with massive price tags. In 2013, Francis Bacon's *Three Views of Lucian Freud* sold at auction for $142.4 million. You could have had three-quarters of *Iron Man 3* for that.

Today, not too many filmgoers have heard of Cedric Gibbons. He was born in Dublin in 1893 and he died in Los Angeles in 1960. In his time he was married to two movie actresses, Dolores del Rio and Hazel Brooks. He had had a brief training at the Art Students League of New York, and he was working in pictures by 1919 as a "designer." From 1924 to 1956, he was in charge of the production design department at M-G-M, and thus he had his name (by contract) on about 1,500 pictures. He won the Oscar for what was called art direction eleven times (his victories included *Gaslight*, *An American in Paris*, and *Julius Caesar*). *An American in Paris* (1951) was a very ambitiously designed picture, with a seventeen-minute ballet sequence with Gershwin music in which the styles of several French painters were copied. Gibbons was on the picture because it was a major studio production. But so was E. Preston Ames (who shared the art direction credit), Edwin Willis (who did the set decoration), and Orry-Kelly (who did the costumes, along with Walter Plunkett and Irene Sharaff). Then there was the director, Vincente Minnelli, who had begun in the theater as a designer of costumes and sets. Arthur Freed produced the picture, and although Freed was a former songwriter, he was in charge of the M-G-M musicals unit—and this was a prestige production, budgeted at $2.7 million, and eventual winner of the Oscar for Best Picture. Even then, the chain of authorship is incomplete, for the creative forces on the picture (Minnelli and Gene Kelly) were inspired and provoked by the glorious achievement and the American popularity of *The Red Shoes*, made in England just a few years earlier by Michael Powell and Emeric Pressburger, a pioneering film in believing that the fine arts and ballet could be made material for a hit movie.

Which is not to say Gibbons didn't deserve his Oscar, but his name is like a trademark, and truth to tell, *An American in Paris* no longer seems that good a film. I should add that Gibbons has another claim on the Oscar, for he is supposed to have designed or drawn the original statuette. He was a member of the inside club and one of the thirty-six founders of the Academy in 1927.

Shift sideways, two years ahead, to another Metro musical, *The Band Wagon*. Yet again, Freed produced and Minnelli directed; one virtue of the studio system was familiarity and a kind of teamwork, even if Freed and Minnelli were never best friends. The art direction group on the film was most of the people from *An American in Paris*. There was one crucial departure: *The Band Wagon* was a Fred Astaire film. Now, in many respects Gene Kelly matched Astaire in his artistic ambitions, and Kelly was a credited codirector on films like *Singin' in the Rain*. He had even directed nonmusical films, not that they are remembered. Astaire never had a credit as director. But he insisted on the way his dance numbers were shot. He would not dance on film unless the full figures of the dancers were visible in the frame, and he preferred the camera to move laterally with the dance, to maintain the shot, as opposed to cutting. It was his credo that this thing he did (with whichever female partner fate selected) was as difficult as it was beautiful. Therefore it had to be shown intact.

So there is a style, a fluidity, a camera identity, and what we call a mise-en-scène in Astaire's dance numbers. The rehearsal was relentless and exhausting; the shooting was meticulous and hardly cheap. Some of his partners wept because their feet were bleeding. But still they had to appear to be in the arms of a god. In *The Band Wagon,* the great number is "Dancing in the Dark" in Central Park (all done on a Culver City set designed by the team). Fred's partner here is Cyd Charisse. They are both dressed in white and the narrative function of the dance is to have two rather chilly people warm up to each other. Neither Astaire nor Charisse were what we could call "actors," but this is one of the great love scenes on film, and proof of how far movie is poetic, dreamlike, and musical, despite its apparent allegiance to plausibility. Astaire was not just the director of the scene, not just its auteur, but its reason for being.

For decades, ever since he started doing movies in the early 1930s, after his first partner, his sister, Adele, had married into the English aristocracy, audiences knew they were going to see a Fred Astaire film, or "Fred and Ginger." The great Astaire-Rogers partnership flourished at RKO and no one disputes Rogers's value: she was an extraordinary dancer (though not as soulful or balletic as Charisse); she was tart, earthy, and a touch rowdy; the famous judgment was that Fred gave her class while she brought him sexiness. Those pictures, from *Flying Down to Rio* to *Carefree,* had yet another contributing author: black-and-white cinematography. I like *The Band Wagon* in color, but Astaire's natural leading away from realism is fostered by black-and-white, and the décor of those RKO films is full of polished floors and deco arenas. Those films were designed too, and Van Nest Polglase has most of the credits—as the studio's resident chief designer he would also get that credit on *Citizen Kane.* There's another name to mention, Hermes Pan, who was Fred's choreographic partner from 1933 till the end—which was *Finian's Rainbow,* where a new director named Francis Ford Coppola outraged Fred and ruined the picture by chopping up legs and heads.

Not that Francis only deserves blame. Just a few years after *Finian's Rainbow* (hardly ever shown today) he made *The Godfather* (which people see all the time, as if they enjoy being a part of its sinister family). Francis Coppola has been called an auteur, a genius, a boss, a spokesman for a generation, a lord of San Francisco. That's a lot of things to be in a package that has involved him as husband, father, vintner, patron, magazine publisher, opera director, entrepreneur for the vacation industry in Belize, chef, and sometimes depressive.

In the early 1970s, in the space of three years, he wrote and directed *The Godfather, The Conversation,* and *The Godfather Part II.* So it hardly matters what came later. To be a maestro or a godfather for just a few years is enough. If we confine ourselves simply to *The Godfather,* Francis took on a picture when many at the studio, Paramount, believed he was too inexperienced to handle that large a project. He endured the fabulous self-confidence of Robert Evans as his production executive. He lived through the rumors that he was about to be replaced by some pliant veteran. And all he did was deliver a picture that for a few years was the all-time box-office champion (between *The Sound of Music* and *Jaws*) and that won the Best Picture Oscar.

Coppola shared the Oscar for adapted screenplay with Mario Puzo, whose book was the origin of the film. But there were so many others who contributed, who served the director or did their own thing—you had to be there every minute to know exactly what happened, and even then who could be sure? Gordon Willis shot the film in so many browns and blacks, against warnings that the film would not be visible. Dean Tavoularis designed all those Italian interiors. Anna Hill Johnstone did the costumes. Nino Rota wrote the music; the score is as famous as the one for *Gone With the Wind*. Walter Murch wrought the sound track in postproduction. Michael Chapman operated the camera, and Fred Roos did the casting.

How much that one word stands for, and how many different negotiations did Coppola have to beg Paramount to accept Marlon Brando as Vito? There was a similar struggle over Al Pacino as Michael. Then there are James Caan, Robert Duvall (in the role that defined his value), the exquisite John Cazale, Diane Keaton, Talia Shire, and of course I'm leaving people out. But every time I see the film I treasure John Marley (as the Hollywood producer, Jack Woltz, the man who loves horses), Abe Vigoda as the mournful Tessio, Richard Castellano cooking as Clemenza, Lenny Montana as Luca Brasi, Sterling Hayden as the crooked police chief, McCluskey, Al Lettieri as Sollozzo, Simonetta Stefanelli (as Apollonia, Michael's Sicilian bride and the one time in all the films where he finds pleasure in a woman), Alex Rocco as Moe Greene. Casting depends on hunch, availability, making a deal, and then directing the performance, though on big, busy films there is so little time for directing that casting may be most of the battle.

Did Francis make *The Godfather*? Well, yes. Would he say so? I'm not sure. He is a family man, for good and ill, and it's interesting to know that once upon a time, with a demanding father (the flute player in the NBC Symphony Orchestra under Toscanini), Francis was the weakling in the family, while his brother August was as flamboyant as Sonny and as brilliant as Michael. If Francis identified with anyone it was with Fredo. And that helps explain his movie a little.

Francis Coppola became regarded as an auteur in the early 1970s, and he did a lot to make it easier for some of his contemporaries to be viewed in the same way—Martin Scorsese, Steven Spielberg, George Lucas, Brian De Palma, William Friedkin, Peter Bogdanovich. It's interesting to note what has happened to those men: Friedkin, De Palma, and Bogdanovich have had periods of decline. Their recent work does not match their work from the seventies. Does that mean an auteur can lose his authority, or just his favored place in the business hierarchy? George Lucas has become very wealthy. He sold his enterprises to Disney for over $4 billion, no matter that he had been one of the original migrants to northern California who wanted to get away from the atmosphere of Hollywood. Few of his fans believe the later *Star Wars* pictures had the verve or originality of the first ones. Steven Spielberg has become exactly what Hollywood most treasures: a great and generous producer, nearly a studio in his own right. He has made half a dozen pictures that are hallowed in the history of the business and one film that seems to me close to greatness—I mean *Empire of the Sun,* adapted from the J. G. Ballard memoir. That's the picture in which he places a kid (the young Christian Bale) in a world that is insane but utterly real. All too often, Spielberg's kids exist in fantasy worlds where "Steven" is like a wizard.

And Marty? He is the chronic filmmaker, never weary or satisfied, a cornucopia of projects, a defender of film, an aid to so many others, our jittery patron saint, and he was at his best, I think, in the years from *Mean Streets* to *Raging Bull.* Since then, his mania to make films has fallen into self-repetition and diminished quality. Coppola is a long way from the man of the early seventies. But aren't auteurs allowed to wander and drift? Orson Welles, long after *Kane,* made films that were far from his best work, though other directors would have given so much to have made them.

Against the vagaries of changing taste, of raising and keeping money, the sanctity of the auteur theory seems archaic. But it was introduced, principally by French writers, as a way of saying, Look, these American professionals, these studio men, these business successes, may be artists. That sacred list included Howard Hawks, John Ford, Alfred Hitchcock, Nick Ray, Sam Fuller, Vincente Minnelli, Otto Preminger, Anthony Mann, King Vidor, and so many others. It was also a way of elevating the role of director for young critics (Truffaut, Godard, Bogdanovich) who longed to do the job themselves. Years later, it's evident that Hawks and Hitchcock were remarkable figures, albeit men torn between art and commerce. But the others on that list? Well, I suspect that "talented professionals" covers them adequately, though some, like Ray, put too much of their life and art into being melodramatic self-destructives in flight from obedient professionalism.

For a substantial moment in the history of film, directors took us away from the regular orthodoxy, the greatest mystery, which is not so much that actors make films as that films are about actors. The enormous library of auteur studies (hardly any of which existed in 1960) has not detracted from our habit of pursuing and enjoying actors and actresses, just because we like them, and would like to be them.

That does not mean the culture of movie stars continues unabated. The wisdom that we have fewer stars now, and that they last for shorter times, is common for good reason. The star system once depended not just on our love and desire, but on the seven-year contracts by which a star was the property of a studio, provided with more or less suitable vehicles, and thoroughly promoted and cared for. Stars had an economic durability that is much tougher to hold on to now when they have to be independent and compelled to seek out their projects and their coworkers. No one said Gary Cooper needed to be a business genius, but George Clooney is a producer with a golden touch. Cooper meant more in the 1930s and 1940s than Clooney does now, but that is because a Clooney lives in an age when the new press is waiting for a star to make a fool of himself, or a mess, and when the public has wearied of its old adoration and likes to be fickle and spiteful. Cooper had a very untidy private life from which he was protected by public relations. And Cooper (born in 1901) had been raised on the faces in silent movies so that it seemed natural for him to be beautiful and noble. Ask Clooney to be such an icon and you can anticipate a wry grin and the curl of his lip.

If you want to watch films, you must never give up on the beauty of the people, or feel sheepish about it. In the compressed history of media and communication, the movies did one potent thing: they broadcast the sight and sound of beautiful people in situations of exceptional and unsettling intimacy. So we fell in love with strangers. Before movie and photography, that had not happened. But strangers, and strangeness, have become increasingly important in our experience.

All of which brings me to the last category of people who make the movies—ourselves. Anyone in the business will tell you that audiences decide what to like, often on a Friday, in ways that may defy every professional guess and every poll of human responses. So *The Lone Ranger* flopped and *Gravity* won a larger audience than anyone had anticipated. To a degree that meant that people were fond of Sandra Bullock and just a little weary of Johnny Depp. But in hindsight it was clear that *Gravity* gave us the opportunity to see something we had never seen before, and to bounce around on the trampoline of space, while *The Lone Ranger* was the stale retread of a tired genre and a clichéd character, and a film that lacked the male confidence of old Westerns, the thing that had distinguished John Wayne.

But it is difficult to do good work while believing in the old virtues of American manliness. When Clint Eastwood made *Unforgiven* (in 1992) he surely was warned that Westerns were passé. But he had the confidence nonetheless to make that fine script, and to balance its elements of a new, doubting Western with the reassuring prowess of the old. So his William Munny was too old, too slow, with his nerve shot. It was an impressive and painful maturity, but then, just to be on the safe side, Clint allowed us to see the angel of death restored so that he could execute nearly everyone in the room. He had his cake and he ate it, a Hollywood habit. And we like Clint, no matter that his private life is checkered and his professional manners can get rough. So many times, he has made our day.

12

WHAT DOES A HERO DO?

Clint Eastwood is only one of the heroic figures in this book. Or maybe they are better understood as attempted heroes. But that archetype is worth examining, because he (or she) has a lot to do with whether we're having decent fun.

Other heroes so far would include Burt Lancaster in *The Flame and the Arrow,* effortlessly bringing peace and freedom to old Lombardy; there's Tom Hardy in *Locke,* doing the right things, even if in some ways they are wrong and damaging things; there's Gary Cooper in *Meet John Doe,* struggling with the toxic celebrity of being an American hero while wanting to remain a vagrant nomad; there is John Wayne in *The Searchers,* so lethal a force of rescue that you might hope to escape him; there's Robert Redford at sea in *All Is Lost,* resolved to go on trying his best until the storm becomes too much; there is

Orson Welles in Kane's no-trespassing privacy, wondering if he was a great man or could have been, and thinking what he might say as a last word for a headline in our urge to solve his mystery; there is even Derek Jeter in that commercial, being defiantly ordinary, no matter that the set-up for the ad is as rigged as Arnold Schwarzenegger in *Terminator 2,* the film where he crossed over and became a good guy.

Arnold is a disconcerting movie hero. He went from being a handsome, articulate bodybuilder in *Pumping Iron* and *Stay Hungry* to governor of Kalifornia (I have to do something to get his way of talking). He did well as a governor because he had so few principles above and beyond effectiveness and looking good. If he had managed to be born in Duluth or Fresno, instead of near Graz in Austria, there would have been a move to draft him for president. He might have made a good or unworried executive, or at least cheerful on screen. People still revere that package in Ronald Reagan, who was not as smart or as big a star as Schwarzenegger, and who became forgetful near the end. Arnold had too much on his plate, too: he contrived to betray a person from another movie, Maria Shriver, who had that Kennedy flourish. One might as well, in considering how to watch a movie, recognize the extent to which public life in America has itself become an untidy, unrated motion picture that has a captive but disenchanted audience.

So Arnold joined *The Expendables,* a rest home franchise for male superheroes who have seen better days and may need a new gig. The organizer for this creaky gang is Sylvester Stallone, but others include Jason Statham, Mel Gibson, Wesley Snipes, Dolph Lundgren, Antonio Banderas, Mickey Rourke, and even Harrison Ford, who used to be the most profitable screen hero of all time until he woke up one day as a crotchety geezer. I realize, just five years ago, I could have been laughed off the page for concocting a scheme for these ridiculous and painful movies. It would have been said that the public was too smart or cynical, and simply too young to be interested in these social security recipients with AK47s. Well, don't rely on the public: on an investment of about $90 million a hit, the three films so far have grossed $786 million worldwide— that was our money, and by my calculation it would have been enough to purchase seventeen F-117A night stealth fighter planes. There is also a video game from the *Expendables* franchise, as well there might be, because surely the prospect of these arthritic heroes shooting down enemies is in league with the industry of martial video games and their kill counts. (*Call of Duty: Black Ops* earned $650 million in its first five days on sale, more than any movie I can think of.) Further, the Air Force sometimes uses such games for training night stealth pilots. It's a small world.

I don't take the *Expendables* franchise seriously (the way I did *Amour* and *Hiroshima Mon Amour*). But they remind us of the larger culture in which we're watching movies, and because heroic violence seems so important to our weather scheme. When it comes to violence, or what is optimistically called action, the medium has turned to an exotic personal destruction that depends on our saying, well it's not really happening; it's safely removed from us on a screen; it's only a movie. The trouble is that as citizens, or as people who love movie entertainment and want to believe in its power, "only a movie" is a dismal and depressing concession that betrays hopes for a relationship between movies and reality.

Violence in movies has been agonized over at least since the coming of sound. The original *Scarface* (1932) got itself in a tangle on whether it deplored violence or wanted to market it like bootleg liquor. But it was typical of an age in movie history that made the screen's "realism" problematic. *Scarface* is about as realistic as a comic book, but it came with the fresh sounds of screams, automobiles, explosions, and gunfire, that fearsome but inspiring new poetic. The picture sometimes had a subtitle, "Shame of the Nation," and it viewed the authorities with contempt for letting gangsters run riot in society. But the cinema has not yet tired of that riot and the genre includes some of our finer films: the two parts of *The Godfather,* of course, but lesser, bloody gems like the remake of *Scarface* (1983), *Taxi Driver, Heat, Miller's Crossing, Zodiac,* and many others. It's notable in those films how little faith or interest the genre has in law and order: in the Miami *Scarface* the only cops in sight are crooked; in *Heat,* there is the movie trope that you can't tell the good guys from the bad; in *Miller's Crossing,* the police seem to have gone fishing; while in *Zodiac* there is an honest if weary cop (Mark Ruffalo), but he's not the one who comes close to solving the crime. As for *The Godfather,* there is one antique cop (Sterling Hayden) and he is shot dead halfway through the first film. Plus he deserves it. We're pulling on Michael's nervous trigger.

It was Francis Coppola, after making the *Godfather* films, who remarked on how the set was always crowded for the shoot-out scenes. That was a harbinger of the theater audiences to come. So, one may be alarmed by movie violence, but the admission has to be made, and the admissions count: we like it. Once upon a time, the disapproving regard for cinema said the whole enterprise was all sex and violence. The pressure leading to the end of conventional censorship in the 1960s was more aware of sexual liberties that were being denied us and those actresses anxious to remove their clothes (the men got a pass). But then sexual behavior was a topic taken up by pornography, and its astonishing advances in becoming theoretically more acceptable in "respectable" households. So it's common nowadays to hear the argument that pornography may not be what you and I do, but it's useful for those unlucky souls who do not simply walk into sexual situations every day of their lives, with invincible talent and no anxiety. Who are those edgier people? Well, let's say the lonely, the shy, the homely, the awkward, and those who feel on the edge of stability. They are bystanders who do not much resemble the leading characters in movies: they are not photogenic, able to say what they think with snap and wit, or "sympathetic." In all likelihood, they are poor, too. It's no more than 90 percent of us.

So pornography is often deemed an enlightened palliative or release for such backward people—while you and I have wholesome and rewarding sex the way Masters and Johnson advocated or as Jeanne Moreau discovers in that groundbreaking film *Les Amants* (1958), in which the female orgasm seemed as refined and tasteful as Emily Dickinson's inscape. (That said, *Les Amants* has dated so much that it is a lesson on our earlier innocence.) The real and everyday situation is more complicated, just as fantasy has become as recognized an element in sex lives as alcohol in social exchanges. Once upon a time as our antecedents dreamed of Garbo and Valentino, so now some people get impetus and teaching notes from five-minute movies in which some "naughty teen" . . . you get the message. But grant this condition, then what can we say about the influence of movie violence, which has gained fresh reach and wonders as filmmaking has acquired computer-generated imagery of things that could not be in dull real life, or which even the semi–slave state of show business could hardly ask actors to engage in.

Times change, more than film critics care to admit. Over fifty years ago, *Les Amants* was candid and touching; it owed a good deal to the courage of the actress, and to the affection and trust between her and her director, Louis Malle. Today, I fear, in black-and-white, that film could look quaint and genteel, just because the cinema was then striving against the barricade of restrictive censorship. A more intriguing example—just because it cooks sex and violence together—is the ending to *Bonnie and Clyde*.

You know what happens there; that film is an item in our culture still. Bonnie and Clyde (Warren Beatty and Faye Dunaway) are partners in a rapturous criminal spree directed against the heartless banks and humorless police. The years 1932 and 1967 merge as gorgeous kids make a romantic wave beating against authority. But these kindred outlaws have not quite got it on, despite their erotic promise and our yearning. Warren Beatty is not totally credible as someone too shy to do it. But the film is cannily written, Arthur Penn directed with an appealing ardor, and Faye Dunaway embodied the horny sensual frustration in Bonnie. (Frustration is as vital to romance as discontent in commercials.)

When the couple meet their end, they are shot to pieces in an orgy of firepower all the greater for the slow-motion filming and the tender, surgical precision of Dede Allen's editing. We had never seen bodies shattered like this or so lovingly illumined with their own gaudy blood, and never felt such a brilliant, trashy expression of orgasm. That ending still works, but in 1967 it was a beautiful outrage, and an audacious gesture of self-destructive heroism.

Just two years later, at the end of *The Wild Bunch,* Sam Peckinpah staged a terminal shoot-out in which the outlaws gave up their lives and took a vast number of Mexicans with them. There was an implicit racial carelessness to this violence: the Mexicans were not as photo-friendly or worthy as the bunch. And the shooting was another tour de force of edited action, more slow-motion and the mechanics of blood spurts and flesh explosions to convey damage. These honorable brutes were also emblems of a kind of lost knighthood who made violence valiant. This was Peckinpah's boozy dream, but it was part of movie technology and a horror in America at the televised slaughter in Vietnam. A similar feeling was conveyed in the ending of *Butch Cassidy and the Sundance Kid* (also 1969) where our movie stars (having dispatched many Bolivians) are saved from obliteration by a freeze frame as idealizing as the writhing in harmony of *Bonnie and Clyde.*

Just as sound had made *Scarface* more insinuating, so the new technologies of film lifted *Bonnie and Clyde* and made it an authentic love story. Butch and Sundance have their girl—or Sundance has her and employs his authority over her in a strange mock rape. But the woman abandons the boys at last, as she told them she would. As for the wild bunch, they assume that every woman is a whore and treacherous. Feminism was thriving in America in those years, but not always on screen.

There's an underground message in *The Equalizer* (2014) that insists on male isolation, and an actual defiance of equality. We are in grubby old Boston to meet a strange fellow, so curious in his lifestyle that he might be suspicious without the all-purpose reliability of a movie star. His name is Robert McCall. He's about sixty and in good shape. He works in a large home hardware store where he is friendly and helpful to others, and he lives alone in a tidy apartment on what is plainly a modest salary. The oddness starts there, for he is also Denzel Washington, one of the most tested and beloved movie stars we have. "Denzel" is sixtyish, too. He seems securely married, with four children and a net worth of $140 million. He has done exceptional work playing Malcolm X and Hurricane Carter. He has had a Best Supporting Actor Oscar for *Glory,* and a Best Actor Oscar for *Training Day,* which was directed by Antoine Fuqua, the director of *The Equalizer.* Washington has played bad guys (*Training Day* and *American Gangster*), but his stock-in-trade is that of a good man who will get difficult things done (*Unstoppable*) and defend order (*The Taking of Pelham 123*). Has anyone ever heard a bad word about him?

So why is Robert McCall alone, and showing every sign of being a neatness freak? It's the way he always goes out to a corner café in the middle of the night with his own tea bag to drop in the hot water that is kept ready for him. That's where he meets a woeful teenage Russian prostitute (Chloë Grace Moretz) and sees her roughed up by a pimp. And that's when Robert decides to do something about the bad, bad world. Like kill a lot of people.

Now, even in Boston, I suspect, there has been a bad world since Robert was a child. Yet all he's been doing, apparently, is selling plumbing tools, reading improving books, and doing his tea-bag routine. But then he's pushed over the edge and he decides to equalize. The script is written by Richard Wenk, who did *Expendables 2,* but it's derived from a TV series of the 1980s in which Edward Woodward played a retired intelligence agent who decided to help wronged and threatened people. In the movie version, Robert McCall goes after the

Russian mafia, who are pimping that teenage hooker. Sure, his mission will involve a few crooked cops, but mostly the swine are Russians, which provides an opportunity for accent-heavy character actors prepared to be horrid, sleazy, stupid, cruel, and heavily tattooed Russian thugs. If black Americans were the enemy subjected to the same character analysis, or Norwegians or Moslems, the film would never have got made. But at this moment it's open season against Russians—so much for the Cold War. It's clear now that once those guys freed themselves from Communism there was no stopping them.

This is not a matter for suspense. I think we all know Denzel is not going to be killed or significantly damaged. Still, he manages to off so many people I lost count. That's because the killing is hideous but complacent—I can see that one might get an appetite for it. As a worker in the hardware business, McCall believes in using the home gadgets at hand, so he knows how to drill a guy in the back of the head or use a corkscrew until a neck entry brings the spike up into the mouth. McCall does shoot people sometimes but he specializes in wounds where Russians drown in their own blood. His skill is dependent not just on special-effects blood, but the necessary way in which cutting allows a film to deliver extraordinary feats of violence. Sticking the knife in in a single take is still not really smiled on, not if you want an R rating (that's the one any child can sit through if they're with an adult). *The Equalizer* is not the worst violence you can see in a modern movie, but it's bad enough, and it goes on and on. In the end, McCall travels to Moscow to get the kingpin and wipe out the staff of his Putin-era mansion before he strolls away. I was surprised the Russian mafia didn't sue for defamation or hate speech. After all, we treat our own mafia so much more kindly.

It turns out that McCall was a CIA operative who wearied of the old trade and retired, but now he's back, still living on his own in Boston, still going to the corner café. As *The Equalizer* opened it was announced that *The Equalizer 2* was in the works. The picture had cost a mere $55 million and it grossed $45 million in its first week. Wait till the picture got to Russia! Denzel was a coproducer on the project, and the franchise can hardly proceed without him. No one else has the high-minded calm that can accommodate McCall's lethal instinct: though he kills, Robert doesn't drink or eat junk food. My guess is that the business and the public will take at least three, and that won't hurt the actor's net worth. By the time that's done he would be ready for *Expendables 6* or *7*.

I'm having fun with Denzel here, not that it's mere fun to ask whether some iconic figure has risked integrity in compromise. This is not too far from the problems of keeping faith with Barack Obama in the years after 2008, and as a matter of fact Washington has been a steadfast supporter of the president. It's not far-fetched to imagine that weary leader sinking down one night in the White House screening room, on his own, except for a couple of secret service men, watching *The Equalizer,* knowing in his cool, rational heart that it's garbage, and dangerous, too, but sighing with shameless rapture and dreaming he is offing his enemies and obstructors without laborious process, and feeling a little stronger before he goes to bed. You understand, I am imagining Barack Obama with the movie, and I suppose I'm doing that because, despite the danger and the shame in *The Equalizer,* there is a kick to it. The lone viewer and the lone hero exist in a rare, secret balance. After I had seen the movie, at about 6 p.m. in San Francisco, I repaired to the bathroom. Heroes of our time, at seventy, need that regular relief. There was a man next to me at the urinals, and I realized that we had left the same theater at the multiplex.

"That was one action-packed movie," he grunted.

And I responded, "I think there were three of us in there."

"I know. Hell of a movie."

This is a vein of film criticism that should not be overlooked or shuffled aside. Bathroom wisdom can begin to be that precious elixir, word-of-mouth. The theater we had sat in was built to hold five hundred, and I daresay by the evening screening there would have been two or three hundred for what was regarded as a successful opening. This was only six days after its kick-off Friday, and I had paid $11 for something not far from the splendor and solitude in which I had once seen *Citizen Kane. The Equalizer is* a hell of a movie, and that word is more than rhetoric. The world and the belief system it invokes seem to me ghastly and alarming, no matter the executionary skills of Antoine Fuqua or the aplomb of Denzel. And it's disturbing that while McCall wants to save people, he doesn't need them in his life. His being alone is a philosophy. It's striking that whereas in *The Pelican Brief* (1993), Denzel's character helped the Julia Roberts character, they never did the thing an "ordinary" movie would have had them do. That was racial caution, nothing less. But McCall is alone because maybe that's how heroes see themselves.

I like Washington still. He does movies that have a streamlined silliness so that I seldom resist them when they come up again on television: I have seen *Déjà Vu, The Bone Collector,* and *The Book of Eli* more times than they deserve. (Actually, *Déjà Vu,* directed by Tony Scott, plays exhilarating games with time—the more you see it, the better it gets.) But why are so many routine films with Denzel so enjoyable? I think it's because the kid who exulted in *The Flame and the Arrow* and the unstoppable zest and virtue of Burt Lancaster's Dardo has joined hands in the dark with a modern president who may admit to himself, God help me, these problems are too many and too intractable and I'm too powerless and the whole thing is going to hell in a handbasket. So, if only for three people at a time, *The Equalizer* is a source of ridiculous comfort that we enjoy even as we hold much more mixed and daunting feelings over it.

You understand, I am anxious to have you see more good films and get more out of them, but when we're watching movies it is misguided to ignore the overall panorama of moviegoing, which includes a merciful appeal to our weakness, our failure, and our passing sense of futility. That context is a matter of fact: *The Equalizer* was released by Columbia, a part of Sony, which is the parent company of Sony Classics, the distributor in the U.S. of such films as *Amour, A Separation, Whiplash,* and *Mr. Turner.* You can't have one without the other.

There is a casual cruelty in *The Equalizer* that is uneasily allied to the spirit of the altruistic vigilante, setting right the wicked wrongs in the world. A similar energy obtains in video games, where anonymous, faceless operatives obliterate enemy forces thanks to *our* finger on the trigger mechanism.

Those video games are for fun—all their ads stress that. But that's where heroes may betray the nature of real war and our status as observers. War is very hard to film. Get too close and the bullets may find you. Most of the best documentaries from World War II, like John Huston's *San Pietro,* were simulated— but at least they were re-created by people who had been there in the fought-for places, felt the real confusion, and been honest with it. Those who have been there know the rueful admission from *War and Peace* that hardly anyone understands what is happening on a battlefield.

So the most heroic and misleading thing about war films is their sense of strategic command. Steven Spielberg's *Saving Private Ryan* (1998) was a landmark in combat films because of Spielberg's rare managerial talent for the advances in special effects that let such scenes be created. So the D-day sequence is horrific in part because of severed limbs and temporary deafness, but also because we feel that human agency and virtue are helpless. The final battle in that film is tactically astonishing: we can follow what is happening, and that permits the feeling of achievement, which is amply mixed in with understandable fear and failure. But the action in that town is too controlled, and that goes with the fatal tidiness in Spielberg's mind in which the fruit of the good war is something the survivors must earn. That sentimental equation is presidential but ruinous to art. It exposes the gap between management and insight.

Graver, more beautiful, and more mysterious as combat is Ridley Scott's *Black Hawk Down* (2001). It may seem disconcerting that unrelenting combat, with many deaths, can be beautiful, but the gun-metal sheen of the film and its removed calm deserve the word. Nor is there any talk of a specious bargain with history. The episode in Mogadishu suggests simply that the American forces should not have been there. The story is made from the American point of view and it is held together by esprit de corps. But it never thinks to say that our guys were right or supermen. The wonder of the film is that some Somalis wave to the troops with friendly smiles. Others try to kill them. Then as the Americans withdraw there is a breathtaking moment—it is the height of mystery—when a man walks across the road of retreat carrying a dead child. This is not referred to in dialogue; there is no crude homily about collateral damage. The spectacle is simply there, like the glorious light in Somalia as the helicopters come in to attack. It is such a pretty place, and such a trap for bravery. There is no scope for heroes, least of all where we are watching. Courage in the dark is too easy. So some of our best movies are made about protagonists who have been turned by life—the guys in *The Deer Hunter,* the people in *Magnolia,* Tony Soprano, and Walter White. But can our culture live with such disturbing heroes?

13

CAN YOU SEE THE MONEY?

It is one of money's deftest tricks to arrange the world so that we don't see it. So it's an accomplished maneuver of the movies to convey a feeling of desirable wealth without provoking fury or revolution in that 90 percent who are neither pretty nor rich enough to be up there on the screen. For decades, it could be claimed that movies were telling us stories, offering us harmless dreams, bringing delight and consolation—doing all those things that the director in *Sullivan's Travels* comes to see as precious and useful. But in asking you to watch movies, I have to suggest levels of geological content and discontent beneath those friendly messages. The screen breathes money, and it's more than a nickel, or however much you paid the last time you went.

To the best of our knowledge, Cleopatra VII Philopator

(69 B.C.–30 B.C.) was either a very beautiful woman, or not. This says a lot about the way we negotiate such subjects as knowledge and women. In *Antony and Cleopatra,* the actress playing the role can do her best. She has to be present onstage, clothed or not, but she cannot escape the rapture with which Enobarbus has described her:

Age cannot wither her, nor custom stale
Her infinite variety: other women cloy
The appetites they feed; but she makes hungry
Where most she satisfies.

That celebration of reputation, or legend, comes after one of Shakespeare's most revered speeches, an eyewitness description that saves every production from having to mount all the expensive things described:

The barge she sat in, like a burnish'd throne,
Burn'd on the water: the poop was beaten gold;
Purple the sails, and so perfumed that
The winds were love-sick with them; the oars were silver.

It has not always been exactly so onstage. Judi Dench had a great success in the role in 1987, when she was fifty-three (Cleopatra embraced her asp at thirty-nine) after she had warned the director that he had cast "a menopausal dwarf." Other notable players who have taken the part include Frances de la Tour, Janet Suzman, Peggy Ashcroft, and even Mark Rylance. Those are considerable actors, but not always cast for their iconic feminine beauty. If the general public had to list their Cleopatras, and if they were old enough, they might think of Theda Bara (in a 1917 version), Claudette Colbert (on a sumptuous barge designed by Hans Dreier and dressed by Travis Banton, all for the emperor Cecil B. DeMille), Vivien Leigh (with Claude Rains as her Caesar), and of course Elizabeth Taylor, who seemed to embody the helpless idiocy and extravagance of the movie business in 1963 and who survived the indulgence of that film, even if *Cleopatra* initiated a fragility in the old Twentieth Century Fox only cured by a modern Caesar, Rupert Murdoch.

Not that I am blaming Elizabeth Taylor. She was caught up in the public clamor of being victim and survivor. As only a movie star of that era could manage, she was beauty and sex playing for happiness, and so much better a businesswoman than her hapless contemporary, Marilyn Monroe. Marilyn was always sighing about what she wanted to do that "they" wouldn't let her do. Liz simply stormed her kingdom and ran it. Marilyn at her demise was getting about $100,000 a picture, while Liz took the $1 million for *Cleopatra* as her right. With overtime and reshooting, she ended up taking away far more than $1 million. In the early days of that *Cleopatra* she had been close to death, or at least "close to death" at the London Clinic, and she had just lost her most recent great true love, Mike Todd, in a plane crash. But she proceeded to digest the $1 million, the riot of publicity, and such weak men as Eddie Fisher and Richard Burton. And loved them all. She also helped define the modern press attitude to celebrity with a nerve and courage that would be the envy of half a century, from Marilyn to Lindsay Lohan. And she was younger than Cleopatra, unashamedly gorgeous, and smart enough to talk to. She was also the image of money, supreme and insolent at the same time.

That disastrous *Cleopatra* began with the usual bright intentions. Twentieth Century Fox initiated the film in 1960. Rouben Mamoulian was to direct. He wanted Dorothy Dandridge as Cleopatra. The picture would be shot at Pinewood in Britain on a budget of just $2 million. This was transformed when Fox settled on Elizabeth Taylor, when the British weather proved less than Egypt deserved, and when Taylor fell seriously ill. The picture was delayed. Joseph L. Mankiewicz was hired to redo the script and direct. The project was moved to Rome and its rolling budget would end up at $44 million. As such, the project was jeopardizing the future of the whole studio, and it brought the old boss Darryl Zanuck back as a controlling figure. You have probably heard that when Taylor and Richard Burton met in Rome, the chemistry of the picture as well as its nuclear explosion were assured. The studio and Mankiewicz clung to this rampaging sensation as best they could. Somewhere around the $4–$5 million mark, the venture went out of control. Fox had to go all the way, piling on investment to justify the first splurge, and no doubt a few talents took some advantage of that. If you write a novel, and decide after a hundred pages that your inspiration was mistaken, you can burn those pages and move on. But if you get to $4 million on a picture with terrible forebodings, there is no escape. As with many wars, the true subject may become the mounting toll of money,

The age of epics was ending in the early sixties, but only after a glory that is hard to credit now. *Ben-Hur,* with Charlton Heston, had cost $15 million and earned ten times that amount. Under the studious care of director William Wyler it managed to seem like a serious film in 1959, respectful of its religious content without forcing it on anyone. It won eleven

Oscars. One of its screenwriters, Gore Vidal, knew it was fatuously archaic at the time, and history has proved him correct. By the time of *Cleopatra*, the film world had enjoyed so many corrections to its old traditions: the French New Wave, John Cassavetes, the realism of British pictures, the discovery of a kind of novelistic cinema in Antonioni, Fellini, Bergman, and Satyajit Ray. There was even a growing sensibility that if anyone had $44 million to spare, donating it to the fragile economy of Egypt might be more valuable than establishing the trade of paparazzi and producing a picture that was more a container tanker than a golden barge.

In Britain, there were sets and costumes left in the wake of the move to Rome, like the abandoned spoils of war. With ingenuity and wit these were adapted for *Carry on Cleo* (1964), one of a very successful series of naughty British comedies and a sign of how ready the public were for pictures or TV shows that lampooned old Hollywood attitudes. *Carry on Cleo* cost about £150,000. It had Amanda Barrie as Cleo and the inimitable Kenneth Williams as Caesar. It had a profit ratio to fill Twentieth Century Fox with envy. A feeling arose that the extravagance of the movie business was no longer appealing or glamorous, but out of order and grotesque. This spirit had flourished after the war with Italian neorealism, with the cultivation of modest but fruitful national film industries (like Britain—with Carol Reed, David Lean, Powell and Pressburger, and Robert Hamer). *The Red Shoes* had cost just half a million pounds; the teeming spectacle and over three hours of Kurosawa's *Seven Samurai* had been made for $500,000; Ingmar Bergman's *The Seventh Seal* needed $150,000; Godard's *Breathless* was made for 400,000 francs. Such lessons were taken to heart in that exciting age that envisaged brave new films on difficult subjects made very modestly. The dream lingers at every film school, along with the accurate estimate that a technically acceptable, beautiful, and powerful film can be made for $100,000.

Then the lessons found a pinch of salt. People still do movies for the loot.

And that's as much because of us as it is the fault of "them." For there was a time, beginning in the late seventies, that the conglomerates buying film companies recognized a young audience who might treat going to the movies as an adjunct to shopping.

There was debate and competition over the part of Vivien in *Pretty Woman* (1990). Meg Ryan, Jennifer Jason Leigh, and Michelle Pfeiffer (at least) had turned it down because they found the material tasteless or sexist. Instead, it went to a young Julia Roberts, who had made just a couple of films before, and she earned a large sum for her—$300,000. The film was made for $14 million, and it has taken in over $400 million at the box office. *Pretty Woman* is a very American picture because it is a movie about happiness, true love, and shopping, and because its charm can sweep aside every intelligent reason for despising it. Bad taste is vital in this form we love.

Pretty Woman is the fable of a beguiling Los Angeles prostitute ($3,000 a week, plus use of the man's plastic) who will end up cleansed, redeemed, properly dressed, primed for education, and married to a successful businessman. Just as *The Godfather* managed to enlist us on the side of Michael Corleone, a murderer and a lord of criminal behavior, so *Pretty Woman* sold the idea of a good-natured whore whose Cinderella rite of passage needed not a pumpkin made into a coach but an opportunity for shopping on Rodeo Drive.

That's because it transcends or obliterates criticism. Its contact with the fantasies of an audience are so direct they cannot wait for any mediation. Moreover, this is a film that caters to all genders: Julia's Vivien is lovable, fuckable, and a dreamy mix of experienced and innocent. Men adore her, and some women want to be her. It's plausible that she could command $3,000, but she has a yearning still to go to college and be decent. A queasy liberation prompts her. And when Vivien strikes gold and finds a man who appreciates her mind as much as her blow jobs, he is ready to give her the wardrobe of a movie star. That's where *Pretty Woman* arm-wrestles any principled audience: the shopping scene is one of the headiest wish-fulfillment passages in cinema.

I am not suggesting that intelligent men and women have not watched this film with disbelief or contempt. But they have watched. The secret to the stardom of the young Julia Roberts was to be like an Audrey Hepburn with orgasms and a dirty laugh. She is no more to blame personally than Liz Taylor was with *Cleopatra,* but even our most serious actors exist somewhere between the steady diet of television commercials and the shopping channel. Often enough, we agree that movies are about desire. In which case we cannot forget that desire includes money, the subtext on the American screen.

It's not that money and its pursuit are urged directly in movies. It's not that moviegoing has ever been an expensive recreation—though, relatively speaking, it is pricier now than it has ever been. Far more, it is that the stress on fantasy strives for a perfection that exists first of all in the glow of the light. Produce stores put extra light on apples and broccoli to make them appealing, and there has never been anything dowdy or dull in the look of a picture. Even the poor are perfectly poor. In John Ford's *The Grapes of Wrath,* the Steinbeckian attempt at realism is offset by the way Henry Fonda is Tom Joad. Tom has had a hard life. He has been in prison for murder and he has grown up in the Depression without health care, social security, or much education. But he has Fonda's perfect teeth; he is as handsome as that actor always was; and he has a speaking voice that has been trained for clarity and eloquence. Such things are not shrugged off or lost in makeup and regular meals. Fonda had been a romantic lead in *The Mad Miss Manton* and *Jezebel.* He had played the president-to-be in *Young Mr. Lincoln.* He was a remarkable, heartfelt actor with an instinct for hard-luck guys (*You Only Live Once, The Wrong Man*). But if you have ever seen a filmed interview with a real Okie, or looked at the faces in the James Agee–Walker Evans book, *Let Us Now Praise Famous Men* (1941), you know the reality of tough, beaten people who cannot speak decently. They suffer from awkward mouths and a hollow lack of pretence. Fonda's Joad is lean and close to gaunt, but he has a face that has eaten often at the Brown Derby, and in every shot he is lit to best advantage. Often enough in life we stand in bad light and do not know what to say.

It is observed that *The Grapes of Wrath* looks "beautiful," and it was photographed by Gregg Toland, who was about to shoot *Citizen Kane.* Sometimes it has a pictorial elegance that seems at odds with the hardships of the characters. Many of the attributes of poverty are there in the film: shabby clothes, beat-up cars, hovels to live in. Jane Darwell's Ma is a decidedly homely woman, but she is supporting-actress homely and plumper than Ma Joads could expect to be. She received the Best Supporting Actress Oscar in the film, and she certainly delivers a performance. But Jane Darwell was the daughter of a railroad president and she had been making pictures steadily since 1914. If you put a photograph of her Ma next to some of the women in Dorothea Lange's photographs, it is a lesson in the unshakable comfort or well-being of movie people, and that is hard to get out of the eyes, especially if you have a nice, small spotlight on your eyes in the big scene.

Actors may be angry at reading this. They reckon that their craft and their identification can carry them through to the real being of a character. So Marlon Brando was a punch-drunk fighter in *On the Waterfront*? Or a brilliant actor working on that act? On that film, Brando was working for Elia Kazan, the director most associated with the Method and most dedicated to psychological realism. He handled Dean in *East of Eden,* Brando in *Viva Zapata,* Rod Steiger and Lee J. Cobb in *On the Waterfront.* Critics sometimes remark on the authenticity of those performances. I enjoy them, but I think they are only authentic as performances. It goes against the grain of suspended disbelief, but I wonder if a great pleasure at the movies doesn't have to do with observing the levels of deceit or imitation—one of which is that we know we're watching actors, not people. You may know from life that watching real people runs great risks. It can be confusing, boring, and dangerous. Twice in Kazan's famous work I feel I am seeing a real person, and it is Jo Van Fleet both times—the mother in *East of Eden* and the old woman in *Wild River.* In both cases, I can't guess what she's going to do and it makes me a little afraid. But that's a rare ability: to seem to be someone born without good lighting or an agent.

The light is there for the clothes, the interior spaces, and the faces of the people. There was a saying in the movie business (it has never gone out of style): put the light where the money is.

It means you make your leading characters look good, and you throw light around to get an audience and to make them feel pleased. One marvel of Hollywood in the 1930s—as brave and defiant as it was absurd—was to put so many women in great clothes. Maybe the designers convinced themselves that gangsters' molls would go to New York fashion shows, while Cary Gant looked like Cary Grant—a trick he never quite understood. As late as 1967, in *Bonnie and Clyde,* Faye Dunaway—an acknowledged beauty—was cast as Bonnie Parker, who looked as mean and harsh as her record said and as rural as West Texas was accustomed to. At the same time, Theadora Van Runkle designed clothes for Bonnie that might be explained away as Texas in the thirties but which also managed to be imitated in smart shops in the late sixties. I'm not suggesting that there was a deal beween Van Runkle and her producer Warren Beatty to make clothes that would sell in stores—but it happened. Helplessly, fictional movies have had the trick of becoming commercials for costume, just as they promoted smoking, a way of kissing, and the nonchalance of wisecracking. We have all of us imitated someone in the movies and that is not far away from purchase. Long before the television commercial, movies were selling tools.

Sometimes, the bounty in an American film is breathtaking. In Fritz Lang's *The Big Heat* (1953) there is an incidental scene where Jocelyn Brando's wife cooks dinner for herself and her husband, Glenn Ford. It's steak, and the steak is nearly as big as a shawl. In 1953, in Britain, where I first saw it, that steak could have fed a dozen people and produced mocking laughter in a rationed audience.

In the same way, the interiors in most movies are more generous than life allows or affords. You can argue that that was a convenience, making room for characters and a camera crew. But it's more pervasive than that. It's a feeling that our rooms should be large enough for our hopes and dreams. In real estate, many houses ready to be sold are stripped and staged. Instead of letting the house remain as it was when lived in (with some furniture you might not like, with untidiness, with colored walls instead of white), designers come in and redo the place. They remove a good deal of furniture to emphasize space. They use the paint to the same end. And they dress the house with a strange kind of "ideal" furniture that looks as if it has never been lived with. Staging is the word and, of course, it means turning the property into a fictional location or a dreamscape.

So sometimes characters in films tell us they are hard up while it takes them several seconds to walk across the kitchen. *Mildred Pierce* (from the 1945 movie, not the recent TV series) is one of the rare films to address money. I think that comes from James M. Cain, the author of the novel and a man always ready to tell you the bank balance of his characters. Mildred (Joan Crawford) is deserted by her weak husband. So she is left with two daughters, the elder of whom, Veda, is a snake. Mildred needs a job and she becomes a waitress at a diner. At first she's not very good at it, but she learns and she will become the owner of a restaurant. As that happens her own domestic interiors expand and lighten. Why not? But they were improperly spacious from the outset. Joan Crawford was an actress obsessed with status in her stories—in *Harriet Craig* (1950) she is a neurotic housewife determined to keep her life under control and her home pristine—and over the years Crawford appealed to women because of that domesticated attitude. It was no surprise, in the book *Mommie Dearest,* when her adopted daughter, Christina, described her as a maniac of cleanliness who required padded coat hangers, not wire ones. Then recall that when Joan took the teenage Jackie Cooper into her bed for a brief affair, she insisted on him showering first and making himself clean enough for her. In such cases, décor can be as vital and expressive as emotional life.

The ultimate décor and purchasable item are the people themselves. If asked why all the humans in movies are beautiful, or beautifully expressive, one answer has been that audiences like something nice to look at. But another is the fallacy that to be good looking is a step to being good, and rich. If you trace the early career of most actors through their photographs you will find how much was done to help them. The studios that owned the actors would have hairlines altered, teeth renovated, complexions improved, noses adjusted—and all of this was long before a time when plastic surgery might be an option to hold back age. Age itself is an ugly word. At forty so many actresses face the difficulty of seeming fresh and sexy still and they feel the pressure of knockout kids who might do the role for as little as Julia Roberts did *Pretty Woman*.

Why is it then that in television commercials for beer or cures for erectile dysfuncion, it is only pretty women who toss their slowmo hair, share a Bud with the guys, and smile winsomely at the midde-aged men who have just woken up. Are we really being told that people who look more ordinary are unworthy? Is our alleged democracy already beset by the cult of attractiveness, and doesn't that actually promote the curse of wealth?

The suggestion of money is there in the texture of the image and the ambition of the special effects. The sumptuous physical realization of films as varied as the *Lord of the Rings* trilogy,

James Cameron's *Avatar,* and Christopher Nolan's *Inception* is as essential to the imaginative experience as the language of *Antony and Cleopatra,* the orchestral sonorousness of Wagner, or the detail in great court paintings by Titian or Velázquez. That room in *Las Meninas* is shadowy and not quite inviting, but its scale speaks of a palace as rich as the costume of the infanta. It's a place fit for Kane's Xanadu. So it's worth considering money, poverty, and wealth as elements in the narrative constructs.

When moviegoing was brand new—before 1920, say—the business knew that its audience was coming from the very poor people. The political thinking of Charlie Chaplin may not bear close examination, but who can miss the tramp's place in society? Charlie himself had known a life of barely scraping by, and he never forgot its sentimental appeal even when he was one of the richest men in pictures. (In the space of three years, 1913–16, his income soared from $150 a week to over $12,000. That's $288,000 a week in modern money.) The tramp knows his place, and is not deterred by it. He may have to eat his own boots and keep company with waifs and strays. In *City Lights* (1931), perhaps the pinnacle of Chaplin's work, he remains impoverished, the wistful witness to a drunken millionaire and the blind flower girl who regains her sight and steps up in the world and beyond the tramp's vision.

Chaplin was exemplary, but he was not alone. In the silent era, there were many films that told stories about people who were living, sometimes contentedly enough, in conditions of poverty (or its movie version, simplicity). In Murnau's *Sunrise* (1927), we meet a couple who live in the country in apparent bliss—until a City Woman comes visiting, vamps the husband, and drives him so crazy he thinks of murdering his wife.

But they have a day out together, exploring the city in a prolonged sequence that is a marvel of that movie moment, and a deeply ambivalent pointer. *Sunrise* believes in rural people, and the audience in 1927 was evenly split between town and country (not for long). There is a hint in the film that if the couple lived in the city then their marriage might do better, though the film cleaves to rural simplicity finally, in the way of *The Wizard of Oz*.

Throughout the 1930s, in the worst economic conditions Americans had known, even to the point of casting doubt on the viability of the Republic, many pictures honored the lives of poor or ordinary people: *I Am a Fugitive from a Chain Gang* is one of those gangster pictures that makes a real social commentary; Frank Borzage's *Man's Castle* exalts the romantic lives of indigent people; King Vidor's *Our Daily Bread* preaches a lesson in socialist self-help. Then we come to the films of Frank Capra in which heartland virtue and modest means oppose the wiles and compromises of the city: Mr. Deeds and Mr. Smith both "go" to the city without sacrificing rural integrity, common sense and common cause. *The Grapes of Wrath* is one of the outstanding tributes on screen to people who cannot really afford the movies.

There was also a contrary impulse in films of the 1930s, and its cheek in defying the Depression suggests how far moviemakers were stirred by the sheer feeling of wealth. So many of them were poor kids from broken homes who had slipped into unprecedented wealth (and before income tax had taken a big bite). In clothes and décor, there were films that threw plenty in the faces of deprived viewers. In *My Man Godfrey* (in which the characters at a society party go in seach of "a forgotten man" and find suave William Powell on a prettified version of the city dump), the satire of wealthy folly can't help loving its idiots. Among all the innovations of *Citizen Kane,* it examines, and feels for, the dilemma of wealth. There had never been such a movie scheme before, and it has hardly returned. As if the spirit of the common man really obtained in the U.S., our movies neglect the actual experience of wealth and its power.

But it is rare for them to examine the deprived life, no matter that we are not just living through a deep depression but uncertain whether we can emerge from it. There is nothing less than social violence in the nation, in the form of unemployment, reduced educational opportunities, repossessed properties, credit card extortion, banks behaving as if run by Mr. Potter instead of George Bailey, and the organic failure of the economic system to sustain our old hopes for progress. There have been a few honorable film exceptions in recent years—*Ain't Them Bodies Saints, Mud, Fruitvale Station, Blue Valentine, Frozen River,* and *Margin Call* (uncommonly aware of impoverishment in the moneyed class)—but as the hardship on screen seems to induce an unpleasing budgetary severity and a bitter aftertaste, so it seems that no one believes there is an audience for pictures about the actual condition of the members of the audience. The notable situation comedies— like *Friends*—show young people without money worries.

Just as the commercials continue to assert that if we buy something—a Cadillac, a shampoo, an insurance policy, a voluptuous new burger combo—we will flourish, so movies are intoxicated with the sight of money itself. Cash is a genre. This began, I suppose, with crime movies where the outlaws treated their plunder like confetti. *Too Late for Tears* (1949), an intricate film noir, begins at night on a highway. Arthur Kennedy and Lizabeth Scott are driving, an uneasy married couple. A car passes aggressively close and a bag is tossed into the back of their vehicle. We see the dread and desire on their faces as they look into it and lift out packs of money—it is what will pry them apart, a dream of wealth but an infection.

In *The Brinks Job* (1978), an exuberant working-class comedy, hapless small-time crooks cavort in a room so full of bills they are like leaves in the forest. In *The Getaway* (1972) and *Indecent Proposal* (1993), there are love scenes where couples embrace amid dollar bills that are like nymphs and cupids in mythological paintings. The Russian mafia in *The Equalizer* possess blocks of money the size of rooms. In *The Wolf of Wall Street,* one of the more surreal and deranged of modern comedies, the tycoon figure (Leonardo DiCaprio) nearly sweats cash. This is all part of the dislocation in which rich people, made of money, are depicted as gaudy rascals—yet our guys. Thus the title *American Hustle* stands not for indictable offenses but a mock-heroic dance with such things. The cultural warnings are so steady, one has to assume resolute fantasy or self-deception in minds that both treasure money and hate it. This confusion reaches across all of our lives, but it is in movies (and maybe Las Vegas) that the image of money is most alarming.

14

THE DOCUMENT
AND THE DREAM

When you watch a movie, or any moving imagery, you have to decide the balance of documentary and dream in what you are seeing. Or truth and fiction. But those schisms are dangerous because they begin to suggest we can settle on one or the other—like guilty or not guilty, the easy way out. Whereas, it was always the confusion that was special—the delicious mistake. When Auguste and Louis Lumière first showed that steam engine in December 1895, in Paris, I don't think the audience was ever fooled. What they loved was the license for pretending. After all, the Lumières had chosen a very nice, amiable locomotive, such as you might find in books for children. It was nowhere near as menacing as the 1930s loco Magritte had like a hard-on in an empty hearth in his painting *La Durée Poignardée.* The Magritte is a night train to nowhere.

But the story goes that some of that first Parisian audience believed the force and weight of the steam engine was about to break out of the screen and crash into them. So they ran out of the salon screaming. There is no verification of this, no documents, no film of the frightened audience. Even if there was, would you trust it? Or were those people simply joining in the game, entering into the spirit of the moment? Sometimes it's fun to scream.

You are smarter than that—aren't you?—though you may like to think of it as being more sophisticated. But how we relate to a scene we're seeing is still perplexing. In Steve McQueen's *12 Years a Slave* (2013) there is a mounting dread. We know enough about the history of slavery or the dynamic of movies to guess that there is going to be a violent crisis, an explicit rendering of the cruelty that was inherent in slavery. Surely it must come in a picture that has been announced in the opening titles as "based on a true story."

This is what happens. Epps (Michael Fassbender) is a hideous, drunken plantation owner and slave master. He is married, but he and his wife loathe each other and Epps keeps one of his slaves, Patsey (Lupita Nyong'o), as a mistress. His wife knows this and hates them all the more. She wants Patsey dead or gone. Patsey is young, slender, with close-cropped hair, and she is the prettiest female slave in the film—it's not fair to exclude that. At one point, she leaves the plantation briefly and is insolent to Epps when he rebukes her. On the spur of the moment, he decides she must be punished. There is no trial, because slaves did not qualify for such things. There is a whipping post on the plantation, a stout trunk some eight feet high. Of course, this is a film that takes pains to make the setting credible and accurate. It was shot on several old plantations in

Louisiana close to where the real events must have occurred in the life of Solomon Northup, a free man from the North who had been kidnapped and sold into slavery.

At first, Epps appoints Solomon to whip Patsey. This is especially callous in that Solomon is fond of Patsey, without any hint of a romantic relationship. It is simply that the slaves have become a family. Patsey is tied to the post and stripped of her clothes—this is clear, but it is not treated as more than fact. Solomon (Chiwetel Ejiofor) begins to apply the lash, but he is doing what he can to go lightly. That does not mean he is not inflicting pain and damage. Patsey cries out in anguish. But Epps is so tormented by the situation that he seizes the whip himself and applies it with such force that he will eventually collapse in exhaustion. Patsey's cries are more desperate now. Her back is torn to pieces. She wilts at the post. The appalling thing has been accomplished for us to see.

It is plainly a purpose of the scene to be educational. Yes, you know there was slavery—but do you know what it was like? This is what it was, and surely there's value in a careful re-creation, just as there is a need to run the footage from Bergen-Belsen. No historian could dispute the way the whipping is shown, and the director, McQueen, uses a prolonged, unbroken shot to make us feel the horror of the situation. He succeeds at the level of education, or art, or moral lesson. And remember that before *12 Years* there really had not been American movies that dealt with slavery in so complete a way. It is worth wondering why not.

But no one believes that Chiwetel Ejiofor and Michael Fassbender actually whipped Lupita Nyong'o. Even in one full shot, the sound of the whip and of her cries are real enough (although we know now that they are sounds laid in like extra flowers put in a bouquet). When we get the shot of her back, it is not her back wrecked by the lash, but a skilled makeup job that may have taken hours to apply. We know all this. Even our children know. And if we do not hide our eyes as much as once we did, or run headlong from the theater in tears, it is because of our sophistication. All of which leaves us on perilous ground, anxious to support the suspension of disbelief, yet trusting that every screen contrivance is a trick—so that we can suspend belief. What a nightmare we have made for ourselves.

Or consider Abdellatif Kechiche's *Blue Is the Warmest Color* (2013). This is a movie that traces some seven years or so in the life of Adèle (Adèle Exarchopoulos), a girl living in the French provinces. We see her first in high school, feeling her way into an awkward and disappointing love affair with a boy. Then she meets an older girl, Emma (Léa Seydoux), a painter in the making, who has blue in her hair. They become lovers in an affair that drives everything except carnality out of their lives. Time passes. Emma is a painter with a career; Adèle teaches young children. The affair slackens. Adèle starts seeing a man; Emma veers back toward a former lover. They break up, though they are friendly still. What will become of Adèle?

The film is three hours long, and it is subtitled *The Life of Adèle: Chapters 1 and 2*. It is not based on fact (it comes from a graphic novel), yet this subtitle gives an illusion of a real world that contains the events. The film is shot in an unremarkable provincial town (Lille and Roubaix were used), often in close-ups. Adèle grows older and more beautiful in fascinating ways: growing older is not a frequent topic in films and often it is done clumsily. This movie is remarkable and it overcomes any hesitations we may have about its length, and its relative dullness. I use that word carefully. Not a lot happens in terms of action, except that there are extensive love scenes between the two characters, enough to get the picture an NC-17 rating in America. It also won the Palme d'Or in Cannes.

The consequence of showing the lovemaking is not simply assessed. As I described the plot, I think it's possible that the film could stand on its own with the briefest of love scenes. But those scenes are as important as they are powerful. The two actresses are naked. They kiss, they work on each other's breasts, they worship each other's private parts with their hands, their mouths, and their striving bodies. No doubles were used, as far as I can see, though I have read that artificial genitalia were employed. I'm not sure I understand that, unless it means that substitute or prosthetic erogenous zones were pasted on the women's bodies. (Nicole Kidman employed that modesty on *Eyes Wide Shut*.) But considering that takes one a long way from the impulsive experience of Emma and Adèle. The film does not show pubic hair and there is the briefest glimpse of pudenda. There are cries of ecstasy and orgasm, but it is left to us to judge how much of that is acting and how much helpless. (In both scenes I am talking about, the quality of the human cries is of the utmost importance.) In thinking of that, we also have to weigh the nature and reliability of helplessness in human beings, and that can lead to the deli scene in *When Harry Met Sally*, where Meg Ryan imitated an orgasm for her character.

But the scene is candid and educational. Some men will learn at last what women do together; although the same men will probably be erotically aroused by the sight of two very pleasing bodies in careful abandon. Were the actresses lovers? Does that matter? Does it matter in heterosexual films that we know or wonder about the chemistry between, say, Bogart and Bacall in *The Big Sleep*, or Truffaut and Jeanne Moreau during their films together? The love scene is, I think, the most striking part of the movie; it is certainly the most controversial and the thing most viewers have heard about in advance. There is always the question as to how far that preparation is there to help sell a film. Yet *Blue Is the Warmest Color* is a touching and uncommon study of a woman, Adèle, coming of age, and the sex scenes are essential because they let us feel her maturation, her grasp of her own feelings, and her likely exposure to heartbreak. The film needs that much sexual activity to show how far Adèle has been altered by it, and to convey the daily regularity of this direct contact. If the sex was not so close to complete, that feeling would not be as potent. Does that mean that every film with a love scene needs to be so graphic?

I don't think it's fanciful to say that most of these questions arise in the course of the scene—there *is* time. So our getting to know Adèle cannot be separated from our ruminations over the engineering and the protocol of showing sexual behavior on screen (while remaining in the dark about what it means in our heads). How different would the scene be if the actresses playing Adèle and Emma were less lovely, and less lithe? But have we begun to complain about the generality of leading characters in movies being so good looking? Following the life of Adèle is a very rewarding experience, but how can it be managed without the simultaneous internal debate over watching how it is done? I am not dismayed by that. I have tried to argue all along in this book that as you watch a film more closely, its manufacturing process is so intricate, and so beset by decisions, that we become students of film and not simply people watching stories. But that delicate balance does not do anything to ease or settle our relationship with reality. This is what I mean by proposing that we are lost.

Historically, audiences turned to what they called "documentary" as they lost faith and patience in fiction films. There were many reasons for that. The Second World War was a helpless inducement to travel, and travel broadens the mind even if its first resorts are destroyed cities, concentration camps, and the lines of refugees who seemed to have won nothing. People saw new worlds, and movie newsreels gave cocksure, inadequate reports of such places with inadvertent disclosures in the footage—one-legged women and three-legged dogs waiting for soup. The dark-eyed wraiths in what looked like over-large pajamas. I can still recall a newsreel for the 1948 presidential election where a grinning Harry Truman dropped his hat on the camera lens as if to stop coverage. By the mid-1950s, Alain Resnais had made *Night and Fog,* a simple, blunt, and stricken account of Auschwitz in which the ghastly state of the camp was poeticized by the commentary of Jean Cayrol, music by Hanns Eisler, and Resnais's aloof editing. More or less, in ten years of peace the world had not seen or realized what Auschwitz was like, just to look at and breathe in.

The devastation revealed in 1945—to the world's fabric and hopes—left some audiences guilty at having fallen for happy endings. In newsreel and in new features like Rossellini's *Germany Year Zero,* the home audiences in the victorious countries saw what bombing, artillery, and occupation had done. The displaced person was a new character on screen. Italian neorealism—*Rome Open City, Bicycle Thieves, Umberto D*—was a valiant attempt to show real life, and common stories as they had been ignored for decades. In *Bicycle Thieves,* there is that heavy-handed irony that the man whose job of sticking up posters of Rita Hayworth in *Gilda* has his bike stolen so he's out of work again. People beyond Italy were moved to tears by the film. David Selznick dreamed of remaking it—in America!—with Cary Grant as the man!! There was an extra irony to this outburst of sentimentality: *Gilda,* an innovative picture about sadomasochism and the exploitation of beautiful women (written by Marion Parsonnet and produced by Virginia Van Upp), is a subtler picture than *Bicycle Thieves.*

Whatever movies did with reality (and they were inconsistent), television lurched like a drunk Dad into our home, boasting of news and actuality and documentary. The legend goes that it was unmediated footage from Vietnam (in color after 1966) that turned the public against the war there. That begs only one question: that the American public at large never gave up its support for that war.

As television drained away the mass audience so movies, in desperation, turned in many new directions: wide-screen, 3D, rock and roll, and, later on, special effects, unlimited violence, and censor-free sex. They even thought of making tough films about difficult material, without happy or reassuring endings, but movies that worked in the way of novels and which aspired to the company of Fellini, Antonioni, Bergman, and the directors of the French New Wave. And so we have *12 Years a Slave* instead of *Birth of a Nation* and *Gone With the Wind* (you can't say we haven't advanced) and *Blue Is the Warmest Color* instead of the shriveled daring of *The Children's Hour.* All of which is for the better, yet it gives up on the old ideal that the movies might be for everyone as it casts the shadow of shame on so many of our earlier films. *The Birth of a Nation* made the business: it funded and inspired the building of theaters and the origin of production companies. But it is a disgrace, no matter that Griffith hammers away all through his specious film about how this scene and that was most meticulously based on the real thing.

Based on fact—just like lies: there is no such thing as a lie unless there is something we can regard as fact or truth. Astonishing documentaries have been made in the last fifty years: *The Sorrow and the Pity* and *Hotel Terminus* by Marcel Ophüls; *Shoah* by Claude Lanzmann; the collected studies of American institutions by Frederick Wiseman; the hallowed reassurances by Ken Burns that America's dying institutions still exist; the brilliant, nagging analyses of our chirruping media by Adam Curtis; as well as striking single events like *Grizzly Man* and *Cave of Forgotten Dreams* by Werner Herzog; the idiosyncratic laments over America by Michael Moore. At the respectable level of art house cinema, these films have found an audience and appreciation. Ken Burns's series on the Civil War was one of the greatest successes public broadcasting has ever had. *Bowling for Columbine*, a rambling essay on guns and America but personal and provocative, won an Oscar and earned $21 million in America. *Hotel Terminus* (about Klaus Barbie) is one of film's best and least glamorizing portraits of evil—it was made in the era when wicked men were becoming movie heroes (just think of Michael Corleone, Hannibal Lecter, Tony Soprano, Walter White). *Grizzly Man* is not just as good a film as Herzog's *Aguirre, the Wrath of God*, but a companion piece in that it cannot rid itself of fascination for a demented but charismatic adventurer. Errol Morris's *The Fog of War* is an anguished picture of Robert McNamara left in distress by political decisions in which he assisted from World War II to Vietnam.

But what is the achievement of these films? For doesn't documentary imply that it wants to do something with our problems? *Shoah* leaves one in no doubt about the nature of the Holocaust, but did it change minds? On the other hand, *Conspiracy*, a modest feature film made in 2001 for television (based on actual transcripts) about the Wannsee Conference of 1943 on the final plans for disposing of Jews, written by Loring Mandel and directed by Frank Pierson, with Kenneth Branagh as Heydrich and Stanley Tucci as Eichmann, is as clear and chilling a film about the fascist personality as any I have seen. The melancholy air of *The Fog of War* did not prevent the bumptious confidence of Donald Rumsfeld in a later Errol Morris film, *The Unknown Known.* Rumsfeld told Morris that he hated *The Fog of War,* because "that man had nothing to apologize for." The point of *Bowling for Columbine* did not deter so many subsequent killings in the American heartland, at schools and malls, by guns, guns, guns.

Of course, documentaries are not responsible for solving the problems they address. Isn't it enough that the matters are raised? But is there a fallacy widening at our feet whereby we look at such films and neglect the many books, the scholarship, and the immense, time-consuming documentary record that such issues deserve? Can global warming be contained in ninety minutes, or does it require a scholarly lifetime? Watch enough documentaries and you feel fact slipping away through your hands like water—not "the" facts, the details of an event, but the possibility of fact. Fifty years after the death of John Kennedy, without being able to make a coherent, let alone court-ready account of the evidence, over 50 percent of Americans reckon that Lee Harvey Oswald was not the lone assassin.

Doubt seems more widespread and natural, though fear of doubt makes some ideologues more strident, and less governable. The larger a topic, the more diffuse or ghostly the material seems, and the more likely it is that "documentary" is simply another genre of fiction in which the filmmaker likes to assume the manner of a lawyer or a preacher (Errol Morris and Ken Burns fit those models quite well). Then there is the passive observer, the filmmaker as surveillance functionary who believes it is improper to make a camera do more than observe, without a word of judgment. As if you did not introduce partiality every time you decide to put the camera here rather than there.

Then there is the title of the most interesting documentary of recent years: *Stories We Tell* by Sarah Polley, an actress since childhood, and director of *Away from Her,* one of the first movies to deal with dementia in a character (played by Julie Christie). Polley was born in Canada in 1979, the child of two minor actors, or so she thought. Then as she grew up she began to realize that perhaps the man she called Dad was not her biological father. The search for the truth finds the real father, and it uncovers a great deal of uncertain family history, spurred by a considerable amount of home movie—and, of course, by the late sixties and seventies, home movie was as common as movies you went out to see. What is most impressive and beautiful about *Stories We Tell* is that Polley has mixed in the home movie with footage she has arranged and shot herself, using another actress who sufficiently resembles her mother. The film is so valuable because it admits the extent to which family history is not a series of reliable biographies, the records of existence, the documents—it is a mélange of facts and memories, the real snapshots and the stories we attach to them. At last a documentary (and that's what the film business called it) had bridged the gap between the facts of life and the state of imagination or dreaming. But it left this viewer marveling that anyone would ever trust "documentary" again. It reminded me that Herzog's man who tried to live with grizzly bears (and there was such a person, Timothy Treadwell, finally torn to pieces by a bear) was a character he could have invented. So on the sound track of that film, where Herzog's own haunted voice speaks the commentary, he is talking to himself in the most creative way.

Now, it may be assumed from this that I am saying Sarah Polley and Werner Herzog are living in a dream—which can still be a disparaging remark. But the condition of seeming lost that I have referred to is one that reminds us of an early instinct about the movies—that the experience they most resembled or mimicked was that of dream. We enter the dark and we take up a relaxed position. We see or apprehend events that are at the same time sensational yet remote. And that strange combination has to do with the circumstances of watching whereby we are helpless witnesses to momentous but inexplicable events that seem driven on (or projected) by a life of their own. We cannot stop the show, even if it begins to become menacing. We cannot quite remove ourselves, except by waking up, and we yield to the curious sense of being on a driverless locomotive— unless, sometimes, it seems to follow our fears and desires. The action of the dream may be lifelike and persuasive, but we do not grant it substance or rights of its own. Let me put it this way: it does not seem an expensive or difficult show to mount—it simply comes into being, like light at dawn, though we hardly know that this is either light or dawn. Our presence at the dream is unmistakable, even to the point that it seems designed for us. Yet it often has a fleeting air of the irrational or the absurd that stresses how far we do not know what it will be from one instant to the next. There is something like a narrative, but it has no laws or logic, and in its cutting—in its shift from one idea to another—it is almost random and spontaneous. Part of our dilemma is trying to work out whether these shifts are arbitrary or intentional; do they mean anything, or has meaning itself been set aside?

Compare this encounter with the two other obvious narrative forms we know—the stage play and the novel—and our new status emerges. In a live theater, the play advances as ordered, and more or less we see that order and how far it depends on people as substantial as ourselves. Cry out against the progress of a play, invade the stage, and its proceedings must be interrupted or halted, as if we have grasped a companion. We are awed and intimidated by the actuality of the actors, and they have our respect. They are alive.

A book is more obedient to our moods. We can stop and start at our whim. We can go back and read one passage over and over again, to decide what it is saying. The book is our object: it sits in our lap or we throw it against the wall in frustration. And maybe then we pick it up again and renew the challenge. A book gives great responsibility to our participation and commitment: reading keeps us awake and it maintains the forward motion of the text. The very nature of the book tends to emphasize the privacy and purpose of reading. Its nature is to build introspection, the way exercise improves a muscle.

But dreaming and being at the cinema remind us of our helplessness. The illusion of life or reality is powerful and seductive, though this reality can transform itself in less than a second. We can cry out in protest but nothing happens. We are there but we are not there. We are having what may be a profound or devastating experience, but we are not there, except as minds that are left to struggle with the questions "What does this mean?" and "Is it meant for me?"

There is even this odd congruence: when we dream, the authorities say, that experience is marked by rapid eye movements. And when we watch a movie there is a stroboscopic effect, not noticed by the conscious mind, but felt in the nervous system—a rapid, flickering in the light.

A great pleasure in dreaming—though it can be disturbing, too—is that the world of the dream (and I think we believe we are seeing it, as if a screen in our head is playing it) is unaccountable, without logic or any anxiety over lacking logic. We can say it is absurd, but it has a casual momentum that is vital to the experience. We are directed by the medium itself, even if a part of us may feel the idea of wakefulness as a corrective or a rescue. But do we want to be rescued? Some dreams are nightmares, to be sure, but the pleasure in being slid along these greased rails is beyond denying. Our powerlessness is liberating; it casts aside all those issues of belief and responsibility, or arrangements, punctuality, and explanation that are so wearying. It is a very basic form of existence, compelling and sometimes beautiful, but one that teases us a little by suggesting we don't exist. The movie business takes our money, to be sure, but then it enacts itself as if we weren't there.

Can this atmosphere from dream be a guide to film as art? Suppose that film's lifelike record is a given, so that it need not be labored after. Suppose the strenuous effort to be lifelike and realistic on screen is a waste of time, and of the medium's miracle. After all, the photograph cannot help but record appearance, and that may be a clue or a signal to the greater importance of the unseen. Suppose that the thing to require of film, or to hope for from it, is the minor significance of appearance and the revelation of inwardness. Isn't it worth noting that the two abiding preoccupations of cinema—sex and killing—have no appearance that film can use? Sex doesn't show; it may all be faked. And murder is still illegal.

For example, the laborious re-creation of the Western is a ponderous accumulation of proof when we are hoping for mystery: the mountains of Wyoming; the snuffle of horses; the accoutrements of chaps, Stetsons, and six-guns; the gruff, laconic talk that is allegedly the discourse of the West (though journals and letters suggest a delight in elegant vocabulary and structure as might befit lonely men—*The Missouri Breaks* and the Coen brothers' *True Grit* are two Westerns that exult in the language of the late nineteenth century). Those pieces of evidence seem so banal, compared with the way two characters in *The Band Wagon,* say, may find a set that vaguely stands for New York's Central Park at night and break into dance to the tune of "Dancing in the Dark." People seldom behave like that in Central Park at night. And they are not Fred Astaire and Cyd Charisse. But when it *is* those two with their refreshing indifference to the park, then the ways New Yorkers struggle through their lives melt away in the face of such bliss.

In other words, the truth twenty-four times a second is there as chaperone to the way running the frames together may promote a dream. I have tried to suggest some films in this vein that you might like to see. So why not speak about *Persona,* by Ingmar Bergman, made in 1966, a film that probes the nature of reality and our part in it as closely as any work of art I know?

It presents an actress, Elisabet Vogler (Liv Ullmann). One night onstage (she is playing Electra) she is unable to speak her lines. There is no explanation for this. Then a nurse, Alma (Bibi Andersson), is engaged to look after the actress in her convalescence. Alma is a chatterbox, and she deals with the actress's silence by talking to her. The convalescence takes them to a pleasant island, real enough to be Bergman's actual retreat, the island of Fårö, off the eastern coast of Sweden. There is water and sunlight and stones on the shore. But in the dream this is simply the backdrop for the increasing zeal with which Alma talks to Elisabet. Alma puts on a one-woman show for Elisabet, who watches with a hint of amusement, along with scorn and tenderness. Alma talks about a sexual episode in her earlier life, and hardly knows whether she was victim or heroine.

Then Alma discovers in a letter that Elisabet is studying her like a character. The arrangement of the two women on this island is like a shell that breaks away to reveal several potential relationships—patient and therapist (but which is which?), actress and audience (the same question), lovers, vampires, ghosts seeking to make a whole person or find some comfort in their haunted world. There is a suggestion not that the two women become lovers, but that they are in love—of course, in 1966, even in a Swedish film, Bergman did not consider scenes like those in *Blue Is the Warmest Color.* Yet he would have love affairs himself with both actresses. He was with Bibi Andersson before *Persona,* and with Liv Ullmann afterward.

Persona is only 83 minutes, in black-and-white, and it is not just the story of the two women but the night of their dreamings and their different possibilities. There are flashbacks; there are moments with a child, Elisabet's son; and there is the attempt to run film through a projector, as if to admit this reverie is a trick, too. There is sadism and masochism, tenderness and power-mongering. It is not an easy or cozy film, but by 1966 the possibility of difficulty was not turning film audiences to stone. It might bring them to life, if they were ready to follow the structures in film itself (as opposed to having a story to recite). If you want to know how to watch a movie, *Persona* is a film to see. For it will teach you that film is an adventure in which you are meant to see more than the things before your eyes. The things seen are not just the view; they are windows that open it up.

15

WHERE IS THE SCREEN?

So if you are interested enough to see *Persona*, what do you do? Well, suppose you insist on a 35 mm print of the film as shot by Sven Nykvist (a master photographer) and shown in the correct 1.33:1 aspect ratio. You are doing the right thing, but your chances depend on where you live. Suppose you live in London. The National Film Theatre will occasionally play *Persona* and they will try to get the best print available. That is their policy in every season they mount, but in recent years they have found an increasing pressure from distributors to say, We carry that film now in a digital version—it's so much easier and cheaper to store, and truly the digital image is astounding.

You can assume that Svensk Filmindustri, the company that produced the film, has a print and the negative still in its vault, and there will be others in major archival centers. If you live away from the big cities then you may have to rent it, or buy it on DVD. There was a basic DVD, put out in 2004 by M-G-M, but while the print quality was fair, the aspect ratio was wrong. Then in 2014 *Persona* was recovered and redelivered on DVD by the Criterion Collection, who got the aspect ratio right. But there's a good chance that you don't know what an aspect ratio is, and you're far from sure when you play a DVD on your home television that you're getting the frame that a director wanted. That decision affects every composition, sometimes with damaging effects. Bergman and Nykvist intended the classical Academy frame and they often fill it with faces in meticulous compositions. Morever, *Persona* begins and ends with glimpses of the two filaments in a carbon arc projector burning so intensely that the filaments merge. But that state of the medium is almost beyond reach. So here is a mass medium for which you are beginning to face the dilemma of wanting to see Velázquez's *Las Meninas*—you may have to go to Madrid, to the Prado.

Or you can see the whole film, any time you like, on YouTube. The aspect ratio is not quite right and the image will only be a few inches by a few inches. But the quality of that image is surprisingly good. The original glow of Nykvist's work is retained. And it's all there any time. So it's far more likely that a perfect museum will exist on YouTube (or some version of it) than be a real building, helplessly limited and large, in one place. I'll go further: Bergman and Nykvist, Andersson and Ullmann, made *Persona* for movie theaters. But was that their mistake, their fussiness? Without knowing it, were they really anticipating something like YouTube yet to come? Suppose one day as you're walking along you think to yourself, I'd like to see *Persona,* and it starts to play in your head, as if instructed.

You can close your eyes and your mind will still be seeing it. Now, is that a dream?

When I found *Persona* on YouTube, I stayed with it for about ten minutes. I wanted to go through that dense opening, checking off the bodies in the morgue, the excerpt from a silent comedy, the intense little boy in spectacles who rolls over on his morgue slab and starts to read a book—it turns out to be Lermontov's *A Hero of Our Time.* I didn't see the brief shot of the erect penis. So I checked again, and I think I saw it, so briefly that I might not have known. But that had been missing in some theatrical versions. I did notice that newsreel moment when the Buddhist priest who has set fire to himself topples over. His fall; his falling. Then after ten minutes I stopped and got on with something else on a screen that had been waiting behind the YouTube screen. I think it was the text for this book. But I have gone back to *Persona* several times and taken a piece here and a piece there.

Cut: in fact, I had the YouTube *Persona* as a panel in my larger frame, and there, it happened, I also saw one of the Rob Lowe commercials for DirecTV. How can I let that cut across a contemplation of *Persona,* you wonder? Simple answer: because that is what the technology is doing all the time. Of course, I realize this commercial may be a rat at our picnic, an infection on Bergman's sacred island. The ads may fade away as quickly as most ads, but it's telling that we can be so fixed in something so perishable.

Lowe is an intriguing figure. We don't need to recount his checkered career, or the aura of scandalous incidents. Let's just say that in these DirecTV ads, he does astonishing work, unexpected, witty, and for everyman. In presenting the upright and Direct Lowe and the creepy, pathetic, noxious Lowe who only has cable, he became a master actor. I don't think he has ever done anything better. So is the result just a cute ad? That's not enough: look closely at the series and you realize that it's *Persona* in thirty seconds; it's a chronically divided person; and the split screen that I wandered into by accident is a model of ourselves and the riddle of our movie experience. We are caught between so many screens.

I might have been shocked once if you told me that's how you watch films—but you have ways of watching I can learn from. The fragmentation of movies that video made possible is not going to end; it's already advancing and taking us back to a wealth of short films, bits and bites, that are not so different from the enormous, untidy collection of scraps of film that existed from, say, 1890 to 1915.

For me, fragmentation was once close to heresy. Of course, that was foolishness: I had long been in the habit of rereading a chapter or just a few pages from a novel I liked. In teaching film, I had regularly chosen scenes and led the class in an analysis of them, without covering the whole picture. Simply for pleasure, I found that I treasured the "Begin the Beguine" number at the end of *Broadway Melody of 1940*. Directed by Norman Taurog, that had never seemed as good as the best of the Astaire-Rogers films, *The Band Wagon* or *Silk Stockings*. But I loved how Fred and Eleanor Powell did the slinky Cole Porter number. The routine has different sections, and I enjoyed them all, but nothing matched the climax where the two of them appeared in a swanky fast tap contest dressed in white on lustrous black floors.

It was easy with a VHS and then a DVD to cue *Broadway Melody* to the right chapter and recline in "Begin the Beguine." I did that four or five times a year perhaps. Until one day I realized I was acting like a lazy barbarian. Didn't the whole film deserve attention? So I ran it start to finish, and got into all the laborious stuff about King Shaw (George Murphy) and the tedious storyline in which Johnny Brett (Fred) and Clare Bennett (Eleanor) couldn't quite see they were made for each other. My apologies to Mr. Taurog and to Leon Gordon, George Oppenheimer, and the *nine* other people who seem to have had a hand in the script (one of them was Preston Sturges!), but it's stupid and deserves to be overlooked. I find it hard to imagine that Fred wasn't just waiting for "Begin the Beguine" to begin.

Then I think of that Buddhist priest on fire in the act of falling, and so many other fragments that have gathered in the consciousness of modern film. There is that man in Vietnam being shot in the head on the street; the Zapruder film, twenty-two seconds or so, so clear and yet the gateway to such speculation and doubt; or Jack Ruby going up to Oswald in the basement of the Dallas police station and shooting him in his black sweater; Geoff Hurst lashing the last goal into the German net in 1966; that woman who comes to life for a few seconds in Chris Marker's *La Jetée;* the planes entering the twin towers; Marilyn Monroe singing "Happy Birthday, Mr. President"; the home movie of your child eating chocolate profiteroles; startling footage of another child playing soccer, the ball seeming as dark and heavy as a bomb, and then the belated realization that the child is you.

Some of this material is Super 8 mm, film you can neither buy nor process now, brittle celluloid that has never come off its spools and which contains a few moments from so many young lives. Or there are the miles and years of surveillance footage, a bleak, gray, unblinking stare from the upper corner of a neutral piece of ground, the approach to a secret, a space that if we wait years some intruders may seek to creep across. And the surveillance will know, and know who they are, if there are enough people in the world of watchers to stay awake for so many bleak, gray stares.

In this filmscape or surveillance state, movies are becoming rarer—I mean movies made to tell stories or construct dreams, movies for which some people still seek advice on the process of watching and seeing. This other coverage becomes a duplicate of life. Is it trying to record every moment we have had, if only to prove that time has been a patient river coursing through us? We have only been here to measure time, so think of an eighty-year-long movie in which a person can do nothing to stop the gradual erosion of aging, despite the occasional flurries of excitement or eventfulness.

In the prologue to *Persona,* the little boy reaches out to a blurred screen on which images of his mother's face are shown, too out of focus for us to read her expression or the focused feeling she has for him. Perhaps she is dead. Perhaps she is his own child in years to come. A boy can imagine being a parent, just as an old man will try to recall his infancy. There could be so many answers that the questions collapse in exhaustion. But Bergman and many other filmmakers insisted that they could find some arresting 83 minutes that seemed like an entrance to time. *Persona* is about two women and the uneasy way they pass from being performers to watchers and back again. Of course, *Persona* is forty-nine years old, from a time when movies meant more than they do now. *Persona* gripped imaginations ready for a film that seemed capable of taking on . . . everything?

That little boy in *Persona,* Jörgen Lindström, was born in 1951 and he made a few other films as a child. Then he went to work in a film laboratory. I wonder where he is now. Did he ever watch the film later, look at that scene where his hand passes over the screen of Liv Ullmann's face and wonder if he was greeting his own mother or waving farewell? The two actresses are alive as I write, but they are in their eighties now. Ingmar Bergman died in 2007—and his great film (Susan Sontag thought it was the greatest ever made) is on YouTube.

All we know of time is a blink. How could real slaves in Louisiana in 1853 foresee that one day a story on film would re-create the terrible punishments they suffered for some stern form of entertainment or enlightenment? How could they guess they would be free, or the degrees to which they are still not free? And how will the actresses in *Blue Is the Warmest Color* look back when they are as old as Bibi Andersson (born in 1935) and Liv Ullmann (born in 1938) and wonder how much it was their characters who made love, and how much themselves?

You came into this book under deceptive promises (mine) and false hopes (yours). You believed we might make decisive progress in the matter of how to watch a movie. So be it, but this was a ruse to make you look at life. The true subject of movie is seeing and being seen—just as it was with *Las Meninas*. Movie will pass as a sensation and a habit. But it has altered our status as watchers by insisting that we question ourselves about watching. If you look at our history now, it is an open question whether we will have the stamina to do that all the way.

I am fixing on *Persona* and *Las Meninas* as key works, and I could have chosen many others. But there are things in the Bergman film that ponder on the nature of film as deeply as Velázquez asks us to consider the larger room of a painting— not just a room in a Spanish palace, nor even in the Prado where it lives, but the shifting, ongoing room in which we observe the painting, and try to discover whether we are the king and queen, misty in the mirror, watching themselves being painted, or whether the canvas Velázquez is working on is the whole picture we are seeing. And in *Persona*, we cannot escape the labyrinth of the film and its screens. We want to reach out our own hand to the image, even if all we feel is the cold glass and the awareness that our mothers and our children are already so far away that they are on the edge of the blink that constitutes "our time." We cannot be sure that we are not one of the children in *Las Meninas,* waiting to come a little closer to us. And we must wonder whether *Persona* will last as long as the Velázquez painting done in 1656.

A little over three hundred years later, in a film called *Pierrot le Fou,* Jean-Luc Godard had a father in his bath (Jean-Paul Belmondo) smoking a cigarette and reading to his child, a little girl, from Élie Faure's *Histoire de l'Art* (but it could be a description of movies, too):

> Space reigned supreme. . . . It was as if some tenuous radiation gliding over the surfaces imbued itself of their visible emanations, modeling them and endowing them with form, carrying elsewhere a perfume, like an echo, which would thus be dispersed like an imponderable dusk, over all the surrounding planes. . . . The world he lived in was sad. A degenerate king, inbred infantas, idiots, dwarfs, cripples, deformed clowns clothed as princes, whose only job was to laugh at themselves and amuse those lifeless outlaws who were trapped by etiquette, conspiracy, lies and inextricably bound to the confessional by guilt. Outside the gates, the auto-da-fé, and silence. . . . What about that, my little girl?

I have always found that scene touching (some of it is cut against shots of a young woman playing tennis, Belmondo at a bookstore, the night sky), yet Belmondo is on the point of leaving his child. In a short time in that story he will be dead, but Belmondo will last awhile on screen, young enough to be brave and stupid about life. If you really want to watch a film, you must be ready to recognize your own life slipping away. That takes a good deal of education. But you have to be stupid, too.

ACKNOWLEDGMENTS

This book owes a great deal to publishing people in London and New York. It began life in a conversation between my agent Laura Morris and Dan Crewe, who was then at Profile. He left that company very soon after I delivered the first draft of the book—I'm sure he had other reasons for going. But later at Profile, the book was cared for by Andrew Franklin, Nick Sheerin, and Mike Jones, and above all by Paul Forty, who was of enormous help with the text. But then in New York, an old friend, Jonathan Segal, was able to show me many ways (just short of starting again) in which the book could be improved. Jon's advice and dedication as an editor was out of the ordinary and absolutely essential. In all that effort, I was aided by his assistants, Meghan Houser and Julia Ringo. Kevin Bourke did the superb job of copyediting that he has given me on many books over the years. I am grateful to everyone named in this paragraph for helping to distill a lifetime in the dark into what I hope is a coherent guide book.

Beyond that, going to the movies, and talking about them, has placed me in the company of Kieran Hickey (above all), Richard and Mary Corliss, Andrew Sarris and Molly Haskell, Steven Bach, Bob Gottlieb, Leon Wieseltier, Mark Feeney, Tom Luddy, Michael Ondaatje, Peter Smith, Greil Marcus, Geoff Dyer, Jenny Turner, Antonia Quirke, Michael Barker, Doug McGrath, Paul Sidey, and the best person I have had to talk to, Lucy Gray.

INDEX

David Thomson has written about film for *The Guardian, The Independent, The New York Times, The New Republic, Salon, Movieline, Film Comment,* and *Sight & Sound.* He is the author of more than thirty books on film, including *The New Biographical Dictionary of Film, Rosebud: The Story of Orson Welles,* and *The Whole Equation: A History of Hollywood.* He lives in San Francisco.

A NOTE ON THE TYPE

This book was set in Adobe Garamond. Designed for the Adobe Corporation by Robert Slimbach, the fonts are based on types first cut by Claude Garamond (c. 1480–1561). It is to him that we owe the letter we now know as "old style."

Typeset by Scribe, Philadelphia, Pennsylvania
Printed and bound by RR Donnelley, Harrisonburg, Virginia
Designed by Maggie Hinders